Che Experiments

LOUIS V. LOESCHNIG

Illustrated by Dave Garbot

STERLING PUBLISHING CO., INC.
NEW YORK

Library of Congress Cataloging-in-Publication Data Available

10 9 8 7 6 5 4 3 2 1

Published by Sterling Publishing Company, Inc.
387 Park Avenue South, New York, N.Y. 10016
© 2005 by Sterling Publishing Co., Inc.
Previously published as *Simple Chemistry Experiments with Everyday Materials*, © 1994 by Louis V. Loeschnig
Distributed in Canada by Sterling Publishing
C/o Canadian Manda Group, 165 Dufferin Street
Toronto, Ontario, Canada M6K 3H6
Distributed in Great Britain and Europe by Chris Lloyd at Orca Book Services, Stanley House, Fleets Lane, Poole BH15 3 AJ, England
Distributed in Australia by Capricorn Link (Australia) Pty. Ltd.
P.O. Box 704, Windsor, NSW 2756, Australia

No-Sweat Science is a trademark of Sterling Publishing Co., Inc.

Manufactured in the United States of America
All rights reserved

Sterling ISBN 13: 978-1-4027-2159-5
         ISBN 10: 1-4027-2159-5

For information about custom editions, special sales, premium and corporate purchases, please contact Sterling Special Sales Department at 800-805-5489 or specialsales@sterlingpub.com

To my wife, JoAnn Marie,
for her patience and perseverance
(during the many months our kitchen
was turned into a chemistry lab),
and to Mary Alice, Johanna,
Michael, and Bridget.

Also to my parents,
Lou and Alice Loeschnig, and
to Mom and Dad Busalacchi
(Pete and Mary)
for their encouragement.

CONTENTS

BEFORE YOU BEGIN

Chemists believe that all things are made up of matter, and that matter can be changed to make new substances. Unless you are a chemist, this may not mean very much to you. You still may have trouble understanding molecules, atoms, elements, and compounds. If you do, don't worry: You are not alone. Many people have trouble understanding something they cannot see.

It is the purpose of this book to give you a chance to do some real chemistry and to help you understand what chemists already know, so everything is fully and clearly explained—all the ideas, scientific knowledge and even the hardest words.

There are dozens of sensational experiments and activities that are fun and easy to do. All have been tried and tested, and they do work! Some involve serious chemical changes such as removing salt from water, taking oxygen from a compound, and making your own litmus paper from berries to test for acids and bases. Also, you will learn how to test a substance for starch, and to cause chemical changes that produce heat or use it.

Other experiments may look more like party or magic tricks, but they all deal with molecules or chemical change. Try blowing up a rubber glove using a famous gas. Pour water into a bottle without actually filling it. Make paper worms that really crawl. You can even watch a banana jump into a bottle all by itself!

Learn about atoms by making a model of one. Organize your very own gem show, complete with displays, diamond rings, and crystal-making demonstrations. Invite your friends over for an "infusion tea party": It's a game, a party, and a taste-testing experiment all in one!

Finally, you'll build a piece of chemistry equipment called a manometer and be able to test many substances for carbon dioxide gas.

Chemists use expensive equipment and harmful chemicals, but you won't have to, and the few experiments that require special care are labeled for your safety.

Assorted sizes of frozen-food trays, jars with lids, margarine tubs, soda and water bottles with screw-on caps, and disposable plastic cups and spoons make great and inexpensive chemistry equipment. It's also suggested that you keep all your chemistry supplies and equipment in a special cupboard or box. Besides being safely stored, they'll be easy to find and ready for you whenever you feel the urge to experiment.

Most of the chemicals and materials used in this book are household products or foods, and all can be found in variety stores, supermarkets, and pharmacies. Some experiments take time, so you'll have to be patient. Even though these are "no sweat" experiments, you should never attempt them without an adult present.

So, grab your lab coat and wash out your soda bottles and jam jars—che*mystery* is about to be *revealed*!

Wishing you many happy hours and successful experiments! Have fun!

Be Smart/Be Safe

You can be smart and do these experiments safely by following these additional rules:

- Always wash *thoroughly* any kitchen containers, bowls, or tools you use before you put them back.

- Don't leave old chemical solutions lying around the house. Dispose of them safely.

- When you see the safety bee, it means that it's extra important to get an adult to help you perform the experiment.

- When you see the *HOT!* symbol, it means the experiment involves very high temperatures and should not be performed without the help of an adult.

- When you see this symbol, it means the experiment contains chemicals that could be dangerous.

- Be sure to label the contents of any bottles, jars, and containers you want to keep, and store them in a safe place, away from young children.

- Read through the "What to Do" instructions completly before you start, to make sure you have everything you need and the time to complete the experiment.

- If an experiment may be messy, do it outside or in the sink, or cover your work area with a protective covering such as old newspapers.

WHAT'S THE MATTER?

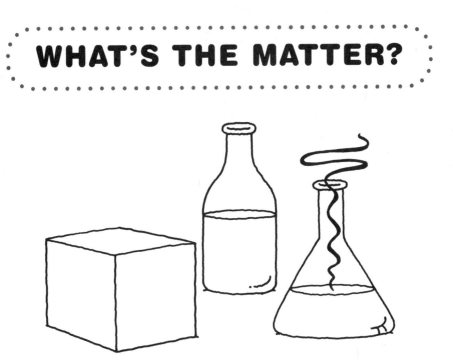

Air, Water, and Other Things

Everything in this world takes up space and has weight—even air.

The three states of matter are solid, liquid, and gas. This refers to how a thing feels, how hard it is, or how it moves or looks, even if it's invisible, like air. A table is a solid object, water is a liquid, and air is a gas. These three things are made up of small parts called molecules and even smaller parts called atoms. These small parts are what chemists study and rearrange to create new products that make our lives much better.

Atomic Brew:
The Molecule and I

A molecule is the smallest part of anything. You cannot see molecules, but everything in the world is made up of them. The best way to understand this is to imagine yourself shrinking way, way down until you become a molecule. If you were a wood molecule on a tabletop, a salt crystal (one grain of salt) on the table would look like a mountain to you. If you were a molecule of water, you would be the littlest part of a drop. The last part of that water drop to evaporate would be you. But, while molecules are small, the parts that make them up are even smaller. These very small parts that form molecules are called atoms.

If you were a molecule of oxygen, you would be made up of two atoms. You would need two atoms of oxygen, because one atom of oxygen does not behave like oxygen.

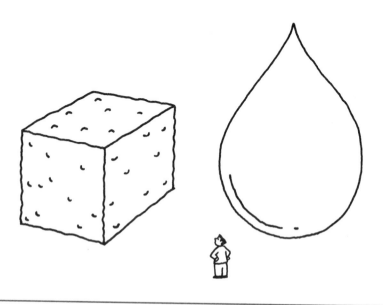

A substance with only one kind of atom is called an element. Oxygen, hydrogen, nitrogen, and carbon are all elements. (See the **Periodic Table of the Elements** on pages 14 and 15 and **Your Diamond Ring? Just Another Carbon Copy!** on page 93.) If you were an element of nitrogen, you would be made up of only nitrogen atoms. If you were an element of carbon, you would be made up of only carbon atoms. You could not be anything else.

Atoms of different elements come together to make different molecules. A molecule of water is made up of three atoms. If you were one atom of oxygen, you would have to be joined by two friends representing hydrogen atoms to make a molecule of water, because water has two atoms of hydrogen and one atom of oxygen. You would now be a substance, made up of two (or more) different elements, called a compound. Water, carbon dioxide, and sugar are all examples of compounds. As a molecule you could exist in three possible forms. Chemists would identify you as one of the three states of matter: solid, liquid, or gas.

If necessary, a scientist, or chemist, could again split you apart, using electricity, back into your original parts. Now you would no longer be water but three separate atoms—two hydrogen atoms and one oxygen atom. The very smallest part of you that could ever exist as water would have to be a molecule.

"Atom" Up!

Everything on earth is made up of atoms. They are the smallest part of any element, and the atoms of each element are different. If you were to take all the electrons in each element and *add 'em up*, you would get a different (atomic) number for every one. (Now you know how we came up with the name of this section.)

Each atom has a central point, or nucleus, made up of neutrons and protons. Some atomic parts contain electrical charges: The protons in the nucleus contain *positive* electrical charges, but the neutrons contain no charge (they are electrically neutral). Spinning around the nucleus, however, are even tinier parts called electrons. These have a negative electrical charge. These positive and negative electrical charges between electrons and protons are what keep the atom whole and together.

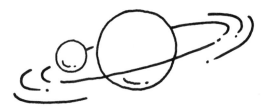

It helps to think of the nucleus of an atom as a ball, and the electrons as smaller balls circling it. Chemists sometimes call the paths the electrons take around the nucleus "shells." Better yet, think of the nucleus of the atom as the sun and the electrons as circling, or orbiting, it as its planets. The orbiting planets are attracted to, or pulled toward, the sun just as the electrons are to the nucleus of the atom.

Charting the Elements

A special table known as the Periodic Table of the Elements can help you better understand atomic chemistry. Dmitry Ivanovich Mendeleyev, a Russian chemist, put together the first table of the elements in 1869. He left some spaces in it so that when new elements were discovered they could be placed on the chart. In a modern version (see the **Periodic Table of the Elements** on the next page) the seven rows numbered at the left and running across the table, called periods, tell the number of orbits the electrons make in each element. Period-one elements have only one orbit, period-two have two orbits, period-three have three orbits, and so on.

Each element on the chart has a number (atomic number) and a letter symbol, as well as an atomic weight. Find oxygen on the chart (second row, column 16). The atomic number of oxygen is eight. This shows that there are eight protons in the nucleus of the atom.

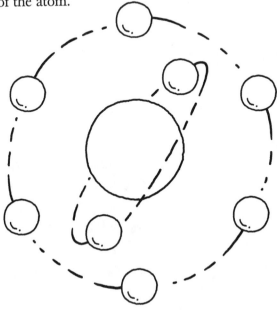

The Periodic Table of the Elements

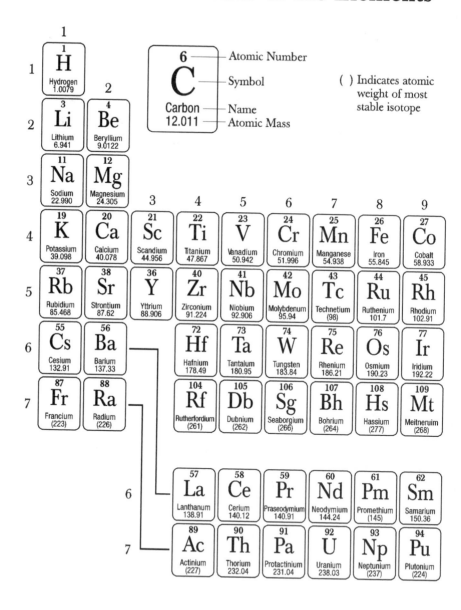

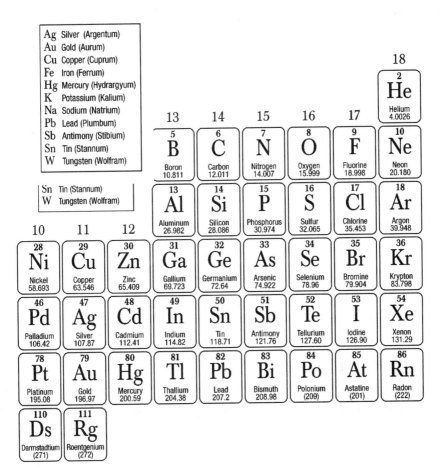

								18
								2 **He** Helium 4.0026

Ag Silver (Argentum)
Au Gold (Aurum)
Cu Copper (Cuprum)
Fe Iron (Ferrum)
Hg Mercury (Hydrargyum)
K   Potassium (Kalium)
Na Sodium (Natrium)
Pb Lead (Plumbum)
Sb Antimony (Stibium)
Sn Tin (Stannum)
W   Tungsten (Wolfram)

Sn Tin (Stannum)
W   Tungsten (Wolfram)

13	**14**	**15**	**16**	**17**	
5 **B** Boron 10.811	**6** **C** Carbon 12.011	**7** **N** Nitrogen 14.007	**8** **O** Oxygen 15.999	**9** **F** Fluorine 18.998	**10** **Ne** Neon 20.180
13 **Al** Aluminum 26.982	**14** **Si** Silicon 28.086	**15** **P** Phosphorus 30.974	**16** **S** Sulfur 32.065	**17** **Cl** Chlorine 35.453	**18** **Ar** Argon 39.948

10	**11**	**12**						
28 **Ni** Nickel 58.693	**29** **Cu** Copper 63.546	**30** **Zn** Zinc 65.409	**31** **Ga** Gallium 69.723	**32** **Ge** Germanium 72.64	**33** **As** Arsenic 74.922	**34** **Se** Selenium 78.96	**35** **Br** Bromine 79.904	**36** **Kr** Krypton 83.798
46 **Pd** Palladium 106.42	**47** **Ag** Silver 107.87	**48** **Cd** Cadmium 112.41	**49** **In** Indium 114.82	**50** **Sn** Tin 118.71	**51** **Sb** Antimony 121.76	**52** **Te** Tellurium 127.60	**53** **I** Iodine 126.90	**54** **Xe** Xenon 131.29
78 **Pt** Platinum 195.08	**79** **Au** Gold 196.97	**80** **Hg** Mercury 200.59	**81** **Tl** Thallium 204.38	**82** **Pb** Lead 207.2	**83** **Bi** Bismuth 208.98	**84** **Po** Polonium (209)	**85** **At** Astatine (201)	**86** **Rn** Radon (222)
110 **Ds** Darmstadtium (271)	**111** **Rg** Roentgenium (272)							

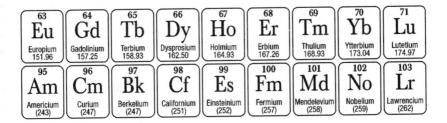

63 **Eu** Europium 151.96	**64** **Gd** Gadolinium 157.25	**65** **Tb** Terbium 158.93	**66** **Dy** Dysprosium 162.50	**67** **Ho** Holmium 164.93	**68** **Er** Erbium 167.26	**69** **Tm** Thulium 168.93	**70** **Yb** Ytterbium 173.04	**71** **Lu** Lutetium 174.97
95 **Am** Americium (243)	**96** **Cm** Curium (247)	**97** **Bk** Berkelium (247)	**98** **Cf** Californium (251)	**99** **Es** Einsteinium (252)	**100** **Fm** Fermium (257)	**101** **Md** Mendelevium (258)	**102** **No** Nobelium (259)	**103** **Lr** Lawrencium (262)

Make Your Own Atomic Model

An easy way to start learning about atoms is to make a model of one. Although electrons and protons are not clay balls (in fact, electrons are fast-moving, electrically charged particles), making a clay model will help you understand what can be a very difficult idea.

You need:
newspaper
4 colors of modeling clay
wide-mouth jar lid

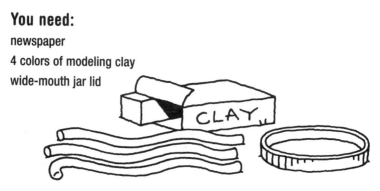

WHAT TO DO:

Spread some newspaper over your work area. Select any two colors of clay. (We're using red and blue.) Now make two red clay ropes and a blue rope, rolling them out with your hands. These will show the orbits, or shells, or paths the electrons will take around the nucleus. Make certain that you roll the ropes long enough to make complete circles inside the jar lid. Press the first red rope against the inner rim of the lid. Follow it with the blue rope, pressed in next to the red. (When you finish your model, it will have a target pattern.) Now press another circle of red in next to the blue rope and finish by placing a blue "bull's-eye" piece of clay in the middle. When you finish, flatten the clay with your fingers.

Next, make a yellow clay ball and stick it on the "bull's-eye." Make two smaller (green) balls and stick these to the outside of the blue bull's-eye, one on each side and in a straight line with the larger ball. Then place eight more green balls in four groups of two on the outer edge of the first red ring.

WHAT HAPPENS:
You now have made a usable atomic model!

WHY:
Atoms can have no more than seven orbits, or paths, and only so many electrons can fit into each orbit. The larger ball in the bull's-eye represents the nucleus of the atom. The

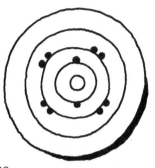

two smaller balls on the outer edge of the blue circle show that there are only two electrons in the first orbit. The second orbit, the edge of the red ring, has eight green balls around it, showing that only eight electrons can be in its orbit.

The third orbit of the model (outer edge of the blue clay circle, not filled) can have up to eight more green balls or electrons, if it is the last orbit, but up to eighteen, if it is not the last. An important thing to remember is that, after the first orbit, each orbit in turn must have eight electrons before another orbit is started.

WHAT NOW:
Look at the **Periodic Table of the Elements** on pages 14 and 15 and identify the model you have made; then add balls or electrons to your atomic model to make other elements.

ISO What?

Isomers are essentially compounds, or atoms of two or more elements that chemically unite. Although they have the same number and kinds of atoms as other compounds, they are arranged differently. Scientists have taken compounds and chemically rearranged their molecules to form isomers and make new products. Detergent, paint, gasoline, and aspirin, products we use every day, are a few examples of products made by this process.

Exploring Isomer Patterns

Now, challenge your brain power. See how many isomer models you can make. Try this with friends. It makes a great brainteaser!

You need:
6 paper clips
paper and pencil

WHAT TO DO:

Take one paper clip. Place it in front of you. You have made your first pattern. Can you make any more with just the one clip? Select two paper clips and place them end to end to form a chain. Use the same two clips and place one on top of the other to form a cross. How many patterns can you make with these two clips?

Add another clip to the two to make three. How many patterns can you make now, using the added clip? Now add another clip to make four, then five, then six. How does increasing the clips by one increase your chances for making new patterns? Hypothesize, or guess, how many patterns you can make before each activity. Write down your estimate, or guessed number, and draw each pattern you are able to make.

WHAT HAPPENS:

Every time you add one more paper clip, you are able to make more new patterns.

WHY:

This experiment is based on a study of probability; in this case, how many patterns you can make in each activity. The more paper clips, or elements, you have to work with, the greater the number of patterns you are able to make. The number of possible patterns increases faster than the number of clips you add.

Pencil Pusher

Most pencils have six flat sides. Number the sides by writing 1 through 6 on them. Place a book on a table and roll the pencil toward it until it stops. What are the possible chances that a certain number will come up?

By chance, each number will come up equally; in mathematics, we say the outcome is "equally likely." Are there any variables, or things that could affect how many times a certain number side on the pencil could come up?

Understanding Molecules in Motion

You can demonstrate the movement of molecules in solids, liquids, and gases in a simple way.

You need:
a small box lid (or flat box with short sides)
marbles (or any other small spheres, or balls)
scissors

WHAT TO DO:
Place a layer of marbles, or balls, in the lid so that they are jammed close together. Move the lid back and forth slowly. Now, take some of the marbles out of the lid and move the lid back and forth again, faster than you did when more marbles were in it.

Take more marbles out of the lid and move it at an even greater speed than before.

Finally, cut a hole in each side of the lid and shake the lid again, and again.

WHAT HAPPENS:
As the marbles get fewer and fewer, they spread out more easily. Some leave through the holes in the lid.

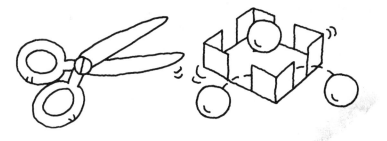

WHY:

The packed marbles at the start show molecules in a solid substance. This explains why these substances are hard. The molecules move, but they don't move much.

A number of marbles taken out shows molecules in a liquid. They are farther apart and they move more easily.

Finally, the few marbles in the lid demonstrate molecules even farther apart and moving quite rapidly. This represents a gas.

The holes in the sides of the box show what happens when substances break away from substances: Water boiling on the stove will turn to water vapor, or steam, and leave the pot. A drop of water left in a dish will evaporate. If one of its molecules is moving fast enough, it will move from the surface of the drop and into the air.

When an ice cube is heated, it changes from a solid form into a liquid state, and then into a gas. The molecules of water never change, but the forms the substance takes do change; for example, from ice to water to vapor.

The Spreading Molecules

Do water molecules really move? If so, how fast and how slow?

You need:

2 clear drinking glasses
cool and hot tap water
food coloring
medicine dropper

WHAT TO DO:

Fill one glass with cool tap water. Fill the other glass with hot tap water. Now, quickly, place one drop of food coloring in each glass.

NOTE: Make certain that all the variables are the same. This means that the glasses should have the same amount of water in them and that the same number of food coloring drops are added. Controlling variables is important to make the experiment scientifically correct.

WHAT HAPPENS:

The food coloring spreads throughout the water in both glasses, but at different rates.

WHY:

The cold water eventually becomes completely colored because the water molecules are moving throughout the glass. But the heat energy in the hot tap water causes its water molecules to move much faster. This makes the food coloring spread out more rapidly.

You might want to chart, or keep a record of, how much time it takes for the food coloring to spread evenly throughout each glass of water.

Three Forms of Water (HOT!)

Sometimes things change. When toast burns it is no longer the same substance. Its molecules have been rearranged by heat. What is left is carbon, an entirely new substance. This is called a chemical change. However, when ice turns to water and then to a gas, the molecules of water do not change. The forms which the substance takes change, but the substance, water, does not. This is called a natural change. Let's see how this works.

You need:
10 ice cubes
small pot with lid
use of stove

WHAT TO DO:
Put the ice cubes in the pot and melt them on the stove. Once the cubes turn to water and the water starts to boil, place the lid on the pot. Let it boil for a few minutes, and then turn the heat off and let the pot cool. As you lift the lid, observe the water drops on the underside.

WHAT HAPPENS:

The ice turns to water, the water to steam (a gas we sometimes call water vapor) and the steam back into water.

WHY:

Ice is a solid. Its molecules move slowly but they do move. When you heat the ice cubes, the molecules move faster. The ice gets warmer and melts. When you continue to heat the water further, the molecules move even faster, bump into each other, and escape, leaving the liquid. The water drops that collect on the inside of the lid are a result of water vapor (gas). As the pot cools, the vapor turns back into water (liquid). This process is known as condensation. Chemists identify what happens in this experiment as demonstrating the three states of matter: solid, liquid, and gas.

Chemists in History

In prehistoric times, people believed nature and changes in nature were caused by spirits and magic. Then early man discovered fire and heat, and how it could change things. Early scientists, called alchemists, discovered compounds and believed that metal could be turned into gold. But none of them knew how chemistry really worked.

Chemistry as we know it began in the 1600s, when Robert Boyle started charting the list of elements still in use today. Chemists Joseph Priestley and Karl Scheele separately discovered oxygen in the late 1700s. It was then, too, that French chemist Antoine-Laurent Lavoisier discovered combustion, or what chemical changes happened when things were burned. John Dalton thought elements were made of atoms (1803), while Jons Jacob Berzelius, a Swedish scientist, believed all atoms were negatively and positively charged (1812). He also gave atomic weights to elements, while Henry Moseley gave them atomic numbers. Finally, the French chemists Marie Curie and her husband, Pierre, discovered the radioactive element radium (1898).

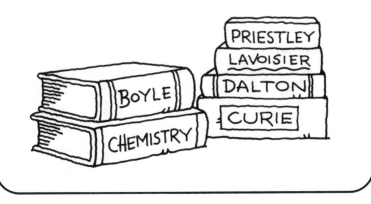

The Water Factory  (HOT!)

In this experiment, you'll become a wizard of chemistry. You'll distill water, or take salt out of it, and you won't need a lot of expensive chemistry equipment to do it. Impossible? Try it and find out.

You need:

small clear jar with lid, half-filled with water

salt

spoon

use of microwave

kitchen mitt, pot holder,
  or dish towel

WHAT TO DO:

Drop a few grains of salt into the jar of water. Stir it with a spoon and take a taste. The water should taste salty; if not, add a few more grains of salt. Put the jar of salt solution in the microwave (without lid) for about 90 seconds, or until the water comes to a boil. *Do not touch the jar or remove it from the microwave! The water is scalding hot!*

Carefully reach in with a mitt or folded dish towel and hold the jar while you screw on the lid. (Better yet, get an adult to do it for you.) After the jar has thoroughly cooled, unscrew the lid and taste the water drops under it or on the sides of the jar.

WHAT HAPPENS:

The water drops on the sides of the jar or under the lid do not taste salty.

WHY:

The boiling water in the closed jar makes steam (water vapor) that collects as condensation (water drops) that forms on the sides of the jar or under the lid. Salt is a compound that will not leave the water (in steam) when boiled, so the salt is removed from the steam. This is a good way to purify water.

What's the Solution?

Chemists study suspensions and solutions—what are they all about? Try this simple experiment and find out.

You need:

2 large wide-mouth jars, half filled with water
2 tablespoons (30 mL) salt
2 tablespoons (30 mL) soil
spoon
magnifying glass

WHAT TO DO:

Add the soil to one jar of water, the salt to the other. Stir both. Look through your magnifying lens at both jars.

WHAT HAPPENS:

The particles of soil appear to be hanging in the water. Because of their weight, the larger soil particles settle to the bottom of the jar first, followed by the medium particles, and then the smaller ones. The particles of salt in the other jar have disappeared, or dissolved.

WHY:

The soil did not dissolve, or mix and disappear, into the water, because soil and water are composed of molecules of different types. These different molecules cannot chemically combine. The soil and water are what chemists call a "suspension" because the soil particles spread or become suspended, throughout the water and then later settle to the bottom of the jar, or come out of suspension. But water and salt do combine. The salt dissolves, or seems to disappear, in the water. Its particles (crystals) do not fall to the bottom of the jar. This is an example of a solution, such as salt, a "solute," and the liquid molecules, such as water, a "solvent."

. . . .

Act I: All Mixed-Up

Chemists often talk about solutions and suspensions. They also talk about emulsions and mixtures. In a solution, one substance is thoroughly dissolved in another (salt and water). In a suspension, one substance is mixed throughout the other, but is not dissolved (soil and water).

In an emulsion, one liquid "floats" in another, but is not dissolved. Mayonnaise is a perfect example of the emulsion. But a mixture, unlike the above, is made up of different substances that do not dissolve into one another or stay together. Salt and flour may be really mixed up, but you shouldn't be! Try this experiment and find out what's going on.

You need:
$1/_4$ cup flour (35 g)   glass measuring cup   hot tap water
$1/_4$ cup salt (48 g)   spoon

WHAT TO DO:

Stir the flour and salt together in the glass (do not add water yet). Is it thoroughly mixed? Add the hot water to fill the glass. Stir well and wait about 30 minutes; then reach in with your finger and taste the water.

WHAT HAPPENS:

The water at the top tastes salty, and white covers the bottom of the glass.

WHY:

Salt and flour is a perfect mixture. These substances are so different that they cannot dissolve or chemically mix in any way. They also react differently to water. While the flour floats and then sinks for the bottom of the glass, the salt dissolves into the water to form a salt solution above the flour.

Save the mixture for the next experiment, **Act II: Bring Back the Substance.**

Act II: Bring Back the Substance

Since salt and flour were so good in **Act I: All Mixed Up!** on page 29, let's bring them back.

You need:

a wide-mouth jar

coffee filter

salt and flour mixture
(from last experiment)

hot tap water

shallow container

rubber band

WHAT TO DO:

Place the filter loosely over the top of the jar and put the rubber band around it to keep it in place. Let the filter droop or sag a little in the middle so that it will hold the water more easily. Pour the salty water- and flour-mixture from the last experiment slowly onto the filter. Very slowly, add a little bit of the water to help the salt solution break through the flour. Be patient! It will take some time to recover, or get back, a good amount of salt solution. Save as much as you want, and then take the filter off the jar. Pour the salt solution out of the jar into the shallow container. Let it stand in a warm place for 24 hours.

WHAT HAPPENS:

The flour stays on the top of the filter while the salt in the water passes through it. When the water eventually evaporates from the shallow container, it leaves salt crystals behind.

WHY:

The molecules of solid salt crystals (a solute) that had dissolved in the water (a solvent) could pass freely through the filter, while the flour grains, which are much too large and do not dissolve, remained on top.

Because water evaporates but salt cannot, the salt molecules left behind as the water disappeared reformed into crystals.

Save your salt crystals for **The Gem Show**, on page 101.

Water vs. Oil

Water and oil act differently, as this experiment will show.

You need:

2 small shallow containers

2 tablespoons oil (30 mL)

2 tablespoons water (30 mL)

white construction paper

scissors

paper towels or napkins

food coloring

medicine dropper

WHAT TO DO:

Place the oil into one shallow container and the water into the other. Cut two small strips from the construction paper. Dip one paper trip into the oil and the other into the water; then place them on the paper towels or napkins. Drop one drop of food coloring on each.

WHAT HAPPENS:

The drop of food coloring on the oiled paper sits on the surface while the drop on the water-dipped paper spreads out.

WHY:

The food coloring, which is water-based, sits as a drop on the oiled paper because its water molecules will not combine with the oil. A substance is called "immiscible" with another when it does not combine to become one substance. The food coloring on the water-dipped paper is said to be "miscible" with it. It dissolves on the paper strip and spreads out, even beyond the paper. Its molecules combine the same way molecules in a solution do.

Chromatography: Watercolor

Chemists needed a way to separate substances such as dyes and chemical mixtures into their separate parts. In this experiment, we'll mix two different food colors and see if we can bring them back. This is a simple version of what chemists call "chromatography."

You need:

red and blue food coloring
small container
2 white napkins
  or paper towels

newspaper
medicine dropper
cup of water

WHAT TO DO:

Mix 2 to 3 drops each of red and blue food coloring in the same small container. Put the two napkins together and place them on top of the newspaper. Pour the colored mixture in the center of the napkins. With the medicine dropper, squirt water on the food coloring and try to separate the colors.

WHAT HAPPENS:

The colored mixture separates into purple (red-blue) and light blue areas.

WHY:

The water acts as a solvent, dissolving the food coloring solution. Because the colors dissolve at different rates, they separate into circular colored areas as the solvent travels through the absorbent, spongelike napkins.

Fluttering Flatworm Marathon

Enter these fantastic paper flatworms in a race and see which one wins. It's all based on molecules, too.

You need:

paper towel strips, cut about $1/2$ inch (1 cm) wide
(make as many flatworms as you wish to race)

a medicine dropper (if you're racing with friends,
you may want to provide a dropper for each)

water

WHAT TO DO:

Fold the strips back and forth, accordion-style. Line them up evenly on the kitchen counter. Load the medicine dropper(s) with water. Let a few drops of water fall on the ends and middle of the paper strips and try to get the worms to cross an imaginary finish line.

WHAT HAPPENS:

The paper worms seem to flutter and turn.

WHY:

The thousands of open holes in the paper fill with water. This "capillary action" expands, or makes larger, those parts of the paper. As the paper expands, it moves, and so do your flatworms!

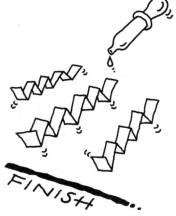

Make Your Own Hydrometer

A hydrometer is an instrument that measures the density or heaviness, or water compared to other solutions. You can make your own with just a few simple materials, but be patient, as it may take a few trials before you get your instrument to float properly.

You need:
drinking straw

scissors

small piece of clay

salt

glass $3/4$-filled with water (to test hydrometer)

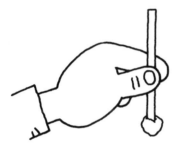 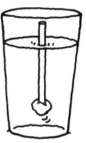

WHAT TO DO:

Cut the straw in half. Seal one end of the halved straw with the clay and form it into a small ball. Pour a small amount of salt into the top of the straw to weight it. The salt should rise about $1/2$ inch (1 cm) in the straw. Hold the straw up to the light to see the level.

Now, gently and carefully, lower the hydrometer into the water. It should float freely and straight up, and should not touch the bottom of the glass. If the straw does not float straight in the water, adjust the salt in the straw or the water in the glass until it does.

Hydrometer Holdup

This hydrometer experiment is designed to make a real chemist out of you. In the experiments in this book, and particularly this one, you will need to control all the variables. This means that all the materials and measurements will need to be the same. You will need to be patient here, too. It may take a little time to get your hydrometer and measurements adjusted, but you will succeed!

You need:

2 rubber bands

glass half-filled with tap water

your homemade hydrometer

2 tablespoons (30 mL) salt

WHAT TO DO:

Put one rubber band around the bottom of the glass of water and the other around the top. Carefully place the hydrometer in the water. As when you first tested it, it should float freely straight up and should not touch the bottom of the glass. Push the hydrometer close to the side of the glass, being careful not to push the open end of it under the water, and let it float freely.

Adjust the bottom rubber band around the glass so that it marks the *bottom* of the clay ball on the hydrometer. This will measure how far your instrument drops in the water. Move the top rubber band to mark the level of the water in the glass. Now, without changing your position, watch the rubber-band markers as you slowly and carefully add the first tablespoon of salt to the water, followed by the second. Make certain that the hydrometer is above the level of the water at all times and that the top of he straw does not fill with water or salt.

WHAT HAPPENS:

In the salty water, the hydrometer floats higher and rises above the bottom rubber band. The water level of the salty water also rises above the top rubber band.

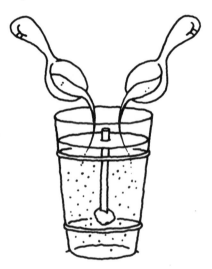

WHY:

Because salt water is denser, or heavier, than tap water, fewer water molecules are displaced, or forced out of position, by the weight of the hydrometer. So the straw doesn't sink as low in the salty water and rises above the rubber band.

C It Disappear!

In this test of solubility you will see how long it takes for vitamin C tablets to dissolve in hot or cool tap water.

You need:
2 vitamin C tablets
glass of cool tap water
glass of hot tap water

WHAT TO DO:
Drop one vitamin C tablet in the cool tap water and one in the hot water.

WHAT HAPPENS:
The vitamin C tablet in the hot water dissolves faster than the vitamin C tablet in cool water.

WHY:
The solid molecules of vitamin C tablet (solute) in the hot water (solvent) dissolve faster, or are more soluble, because heat energy from the water causes the molecules in the vitamin C tablet to vibrate and move farther apart. Without heat energy, no such sudden change can occur in the cool water.

. . . .

Tip of the Iceberg

If all the icebergs in the seas were to melt, would the sea level rise? This very simple experiment will give us the answer, and it's based on a very important compound chemists study—water!

You need:

glass 6 to 8 ice cubes

warm water

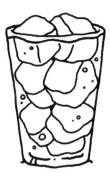

WHAT TO DO:

Place as many ice cubes as you can into a glass; then fill the glass to the brim with warm water. Wait.

WHAT HAPPENS:

When the ice cubes melt, the water does not overflow.

WHY:

The ice cubes simply displaced the water in the glass, or the amount of ice that melted was exactly equal to the mass of the ice cubes below the water. Like the ice cubes in the glass, the main part of an iceberg is under water. If all the icebergs were to melt, as did the ice cubes in our experiment, the sea level would remain the same.

....

Air Is Real

How do you know air is real? Since it is invisible, you certainly can't see it. Can you prove it really exists? The following experiment will give you the answer. Roll up your sleeves for this one!

You need:

drinking glass

stiff rubber pad, such as a mouse pad, or plastic lid

deep basin or pot filled almost to the top with water

medicine dropper

WHAT TO DO:

Fill the glass with water. Put the rubber pad over the mouth of the glass. Hold it in place with your hand. Now, carefully turn the glass upside down and place it under the water in the pot or basin until it is completely under the surface. Do not remove the pad until the glass is completely under the water and touching the bottom of the pot.

Observe the water level in the glass. Tilt the glass to one side and carefully place the empty medicine dropper under it. Squeeze the dropper. Remove the dropper from the pot and squeeze the water out of it. Repeat what you did before (squeezing the empty dropper under the glass). Do this several times. You'll know you're doing this experiment correctly when, after squeezing the dropper, you see bubbles entering the glass of water.

WHAT HAPPENS:

Air bubbles move up the inside of the glass and the water level in the glass gets lower.

WHY:

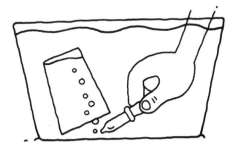

Air was in the medicine dropper when you squeezed it. The bubbles on the side of the glass were the air forced out of the dropper. As you "pumped" air into the glass with the dropper over and over, you saw the water level in the glass go down. Since the air had to go somewhere, it displaced some of the water, forcing it out of the glass. Now you know that air is real. It takes up space.

Pop Top

When its air is warmed, will a pop bottle pop its top?

You need:
plastic 2-liter soda bottle with cap

WHAT TO DO:

Wet the cap of the soda bottle and set it upside down on top of the container. Gently place your hands around the bottle. Hold it, but do not squeeze it.

WHAT HAPPENS:

The cap jumps or pops off the bottle.

WHY:

When you place your hands around the bottle, you warm the air inside it, and the molecules of warm air expand and try to escape. The wet cap at first acts as a seal and keeps the air in place, but eventually some of it manages to escape and pushes the lid to the side or off the top of the bottle. If the cap doesn't fall and you keep your hands placed around the bottle, you can continue to make it jump.

Banana Split HOT!

Can you place a banana in a bottle without using your hands? Amaze your friends with this party-trick science experiment. Watch carefully, before the banana is quicker than the eye in this split-second surprise. Moreover, it all has to do with molecules and air.

You need:

funnel

a clean, long, narrow bottle
(with banana-size mouth)

dish towel

teakettle with boiling water

$1/2$ banana, peeled

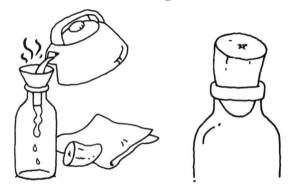

WHAT TO DO:

Set the bottle in the sink. Put the funnel into the bottle neck and carefully fill the bottle almost to the top with boiling water (adult help recommended). Remove the funnel. Wrap a dish towel around the bottle and gently swirl the water around; then pour it out. Quickly fit the pointed end of the half-banana downward into the bottle neck so that it makes an airtight plug. (Watch the variables—the size of the banana and bottle neck, the amount of hot water, the time it takes—and be patient! You may have to do this experiment several times to get it right, but you will succeed!)

WHAT HAPPENS:

The banana is sucked down into the bottom of the bottle.

WHY:

The heat from the boiling water causes the air inside the bottle to expand, forcing some of it out. When the banana is placed into the mouth of the bottle and the cooling air inside the bottle shrinks again, the air pressure inside is reduced, and the greater air pressure outside shoves the banana ahead of it into the bottle. This gives you an idea of what happens when air is removed from a space and nothing takes its place (partial vacuum). Just small differences in air pressure can cause things to move.

WHAT NOW:

You want to recycle the bottle, but the banana is inside it! What can you do?

Just wait a few days. Let the bacteria in the banana do their chemistry work. Bacteria give off enzymes that break down proteins and starches. The banana will eventually change chemically (ferment) and soften enough to be removed easily.

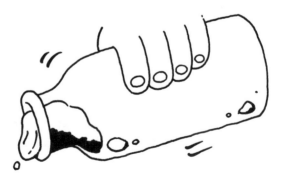

Air Force

Molecules of air not only take up space, they can even stop water from entering a bottle.

You need:

funnel

small, narrow-neck bottle

small piece of clay

glass of water

WHAT TO DO:

Place the funnel in the bottle. Roll a small clay rope and fit it around the funnel in the bottle neck. Press the clay rope firmly around the funnel to seal it completely, making the bottle airtight. Now, slowly pour a small amount of water into the bottle, a little at a time. Continue to do this until you've completely emptied the glass.

WHAT HAPPENS:

At first, water will enter the bottle, but as you continue to pour the water, less will enter. Finally, the funnel will fill up with water and none will enter the bottle.

WHY:

The molecules of air in the closed bottle will eventually press together and take up all the space there is, and so will stop any more water from entering.

Dry Goods

Molecules of air can even stop paper from getting wet in a glass of water.

You need:

napkin or paper towel
small drinking glass
glass bowl
water

WHAT TO DO:

Crumple the paper and place it in the bottom of the glass. Make certain it is tight so that the paper will not fall out. Fill the bowl with water. Now, turn the glass upside down over the bowl and lower it until it touches the bottom of the bowl. Lift the glass straight up out of the bowl. Continue to keep it upside down as you dry around and inside the rim of it. Now, take the paper out of the glass.

WHAT HAPPENS:

The paper inside the glass remains dry.

WHY:

When the glass is pushed into the water, the molecules of air do not escape but instead are pressed together and act as a shield between the water and the paper. Some water enters the glass but not enough to wet the paper. The molecules of air take up enough space to block it.

Soft-Touch Soapsuds

Did you know that water can be hard or soft? What effect does that have on soapsuds? (You'll use two chemical compounds again, Epsom salts and washing soda, or sodium carbonate.)

You need:

3 jars or glasses of equal size

warm tap water

1 tablespoon (15 mL) Epsom salts
(available in supermarket or pharmacy)

1 tablespoon (15 mL) washing soda

3 teaspoons (15 mL) dishwashing liquid

spoon

WHAT TO DO:

Fill all three containers with warm water. Pour the Epsom salts in one container. Stir the solution thoroughly. Do the same with the washing soda in the second container. Add a teaspoon of dishwashing liquid to each container, including the one with plain tap water. Stir each of the solutions and try to make suds.

WHAT HAPPENS:

Suds form in the water with the washing soda, but few form in the water with the Epsom salts.

WHY:

Washing soda "softens" water, while Epsom salts is a mineral that makes water "hard."

Tap water often contains calcium salts, which stops soap from making suds. If water has a lot of salts, it is called "hard." Washing soda "softens" or neutralizes the calcium salts in the water and forms a solid substance, called a precipitate, that falls to the bottom of a solution when a chemical reaction takes place. (This is where that ring comes from in the bathtub.)

Epsom salts is a mineral that makes water hard. That is why you couldn't get soapsuds to form. Did your plain tap water make suds? Is your tap water hard or soft, or in between? Now empty the solutions in each glass. What do you see on the sides of the Epsom salts and washing soda containers?

HERE'S SUPERMAN, BUT WHERE'S CLARK?

When Clark Kent changes into Superman, he is no longer the same person. Clark is nowhere to be seen when Superman flies through the air.

In some ways, chemical reactions or changes are like Clark and Superman. After a chemical change or reaction, the molecules of a substance are no longer the same. The substance has changed completely.

Chemical changes occur every day, everywhere—even our bodies are chemical factories. The food we eat combines with oxygen and causes a chemical change that releases heat and energy. Other chemical changes include the burning of coal, oil, gasoline, and wood. Chemists also produce chemical changes that make new products such as cloth, plastics, cleaners, paints, and foods.

In this chapter, we'll take oxygen from a compound, produce carbon dioxide from other substances, and combine two substances to make a new chemical compound called a precipitate.

These are just a few of the many exciting experiments that involve rearranging atoms to make new substances.

Very Berry Litmus Paper

Here is your chance to make your own litmus paper to test for acids and bases. (Bases are also called alkalis.) You'll find it *berry* easy!

You need:

$1/_2$ cup (75 g) of berries, such as blackberries, blueberries, or strawberries (use only one type, however)

small bowl

fork

water

small strips cut from white construction paper

teaspoon

paper towels

WHAT TO DO:

Remove any stems and place the berries in a bowl. Mash the berries with the fork until they look like jam. Add a little water to thin the juice. Dip the paper strips in the juice and spoon the juice over them until they are well coated. Slide the strips between your thumb and finger to remove the pulp. Place the strips on paper towels to dry. When they are dry, pick off any big pieces of pulp or berry skins you missed and your Very Berry Litmus Paper is ready for use.

What Do the Color Changes Mean?

Purple blackberry litmus turns pinkish red in acids and deep purple in bases, or alkali compounds. These strips work best for litmus testing because they show the most change.

• Purple blueberry litmus turns reddish purple in acids and light bluish purple in bases.

• Pink strawberry (although not as noticeable as the other two) turns bright pink in acids and light pinkish blue in bases.

Thoroughly confused? Not to worry! We can tell you how to remember this easily: The paper that has more red in it is reacting to acids, while the paper that has more blue in it is reacting to bases.

Litmus Lotto

Are you ready to test your homemade Very Berry Litmus Paper? By dipping the paper into different solutions, you can find out if the substance is acid or base (a substance that can dissolve in water and weaken acids).

You need:

$1/2$ cup (120 mL) water

3 tablespoons (45 mL) dishwashing liquid

2 small containers, one with lid

$1/4$ cup (60 mL) vinegar

2 Very Berry Litmus Strips

paper and pencil

some newspaper

WHAT TO DO:

First read **What Do the Color Changes Mean?** on page 51 before continuing. Put the water and dishwashing liquid into the container with a lid, close it up and shake to mix well. Put the vinegar into the other container. Dip strips of litmus paper into the solution. Hypothesize, or guess, if the color change will show whether that solution is acid or alkali. Write down the name of the solution (dishwashing liquid and vinegar), and record your answers. Now dry the strips of litmus on the news-paper (about five minutes) and label them as to what solutions they were dipped into and what color changes were noticed. Was your hypothesis, or guess, correct?

WHAT HAPPENS:

The litmus dipped into the vinegar has more red in it. The lit-mus dipped into the soapy water has more blue in it.

WHY:

Vinegar is an acetic acid, but soapy water is an alkali com-pound, or base. The berry-colored litmus papers are positive tests to determine which substances are acids or bases.

NOTE: Keep containers, litmus paper, pencil and paper for the next experiment.

More Litmus Lotto

Are you ready to do some more testing with litmus paper? Basically, you'll be doing the same thing as you did in **Litmus Lotto** (page 51) but with different substances.

You need:

2 paper strips of Very Berry litmus

$1/2$ cup (120 mL) water,
with 2 or 3 squirts of window cleaner with ammonia.

Be careful! This solution can be harmful!

Dispose of it carefully when finished!

$1/4$ cup (60mL) lemon juice

WHAT TO DO:

Dip the litmus strips and record your guesses and the results of the test as you did for **Litmus Lotto**.

WHAT HAPPENS:

The litmus that was dipped into the lemon juice will have more red in it, but the one that was dipped into the window cleaner mixture will show more blue.

WHY:

Lemon juice is another acid, called citric acid, but the ammonia solution is an alkali compound. Can you guess what other fruits may have citric acid, and test your hypothesis?

Still More Litmus Lotto

Use your Very Berry Litmus Paper again to test your tap water, soil, swimming pool or pond water, even your saliva.

You need:

containers
(small jars paper
or Styrofoam cups,
margarine tubs)

Very Berry Litmus Strips

testing samples:
backyard soil with water
tap water
local pond, lake, or river water
saliva
Whatever else you like

WHAT TO DO:

Dip the strips of litmus paper into the samples. (See "What to Do" under **Litmus Lotto**, page 51.)

WHAT HAPPENS:

The strips will change color depending on whether the samples are more acid or alkali.

WHY:

The litmus papers are positive tests for the acids or bases in substances. (See **What Do the Color Changes Mean?** on page 51.)

Starch Search

How do you know if certain substances contain starch? Starch, a substance found in plants, gives us energy. Chemists are especially interested in starch because it is a compound made up of carbon, hydrogen, and oxygen. This experiment will help us find out if a solution has starch.

You need:

half-liter plastic bottle
 or similar container,
 $^3/_4$ filled with water

2 teaspoons (10 mL) cornstarch
medicine dropper
tincture of iodine

NOTE: Iodine is a poisonous chemical. Get adult help and dispose of this experiment carefully when finished! Wash thoroughly any utensils you wish to keep!

WHAT TO DO:

Spoon the cornstarch into the bottle of water. Use the medicine dropper to add 20 drops of iodine to the water. Gently swirl the contents around and then let the solution "rest" for a few minutes.

WHAT HAPPENS:

The water turns dark blue or purple.

WHY:

Iodine is a good test for starch. It combines chemically with starch—in this case cornstarch—to produce the dark blue color. Chemists regularly use iodine for this purpose.

Look up iodine on the **Periodic Table of the Elements** chart on pages 14 and 15. What does it tell you about the iodine atom?

The Great Oxygen Escape

If you can add an atom, can you subtract one—or release an element from a compound? Watch carefully! Oxygen will actually escape before your very eyes in this electric and thrilling experiment.

You need:

modeling clay

small bottle or jar
(to hold hydrogen peroxide)

1 tablespoon (15 mL)
hydrogen peroxide

magnifying glass

small amount of rust
(scraped from old iron object)

small, deep container or bowl
filled with hot tap water
(to submerge small bottle)

WHAT TO DO:

Stick a small piece of modeling clay on the bottom of the bottle. (This will anchor the bottle down and keep it steady under the water.) Put the hydrogen peroxide into the bottle and then add the iron rust. Lower the container into the bowl of hot water and press it against the bottom. Watch the bottle closely through the magnifying glass.

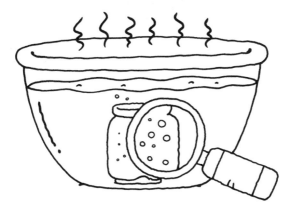

WHAT HAPPENS:

Many small bubbles come from the jar of hydrogen peroxide.

WHY:

A molecule of hydrogen peroxide (H_2O_2) contains one more atom of oxygen than a molecule of water (H_2O). When you drop the iron rust into the peroxide and place the container into the hot water, a chemical change takes place. The bubbles you see in the peroxide solution are really groups of those "extra" oxygen atoms being released from the hydrogen peroxide compound.

Plant Power

Plants don't eat. They make their own food from the energy of the sun (a process called photosynthesis). They change water and carbon dioxide into glucose (a kind of sugar) and oxygen. The sugar is then turned into starch. Both the sugar and the starch help plants live.

Flour Power

Chemists understand proteins as chemical compounds. A protein called gluten is found in grains, especially wheat. Now let's see how we can put the gluten in bread to work as a chemical.

You need:
paper and pencil
slice of rye bread

WHAT TO DO:
With the pencil, scribble two or three dark areas on the paper. Tear off a piece of rye bread and rub it hard across the scribbled areas.

WHAT HAPPENS:
The bread works like an eraser and cleans the paper.

WHY:
The gluten protein in the rye bread is sticky. When you rub the bread across the dark penciled areas, you lift the marks from the paper using the sticky protein.

Rye Clean

You know now why scientists use gluten in substances to clean things. But what things? The sticky protein in bread will erase pencil marks, but will it remove other spots? Soil your fingers with dirt, oil, or jam. Rub your fingers on the paper to make soiled areas on it. Now test how well the rye bread cleans these.

Color Me Gone

You need:

cup of dark tea
  (hot or iced)

1 lemon, cut into quarters

WHAT TO DO:

Squeeze a little of the first piece of lemon into the tea. Continue to increase the amount of lemon in the tea until all of the quarters are fully squeezed and used up.

WHAT HAPPENS:

The lemon causes the color of the tea to completely fade.

WHY:

The citric acid in lemon is a bleaching agent that reacts chemically with the color in the tea to lighten it.

Soapsud Derby

How do laundry detergents work?

You need:

2 medium-size jars, one with lid, filled with water

pieces of white string

1 tablespoon (15 mL) liquid or powdered laundry detergent

WHAT TO DO:

Add the detergent to the jar with a lid. Screw the lid on, shake the jar, and remove the lid. The other jar will contain only plain water. Now drop three or four pieces of string into each jar and watch what happens to the strings.

WHAT HAPPENS:

The strings in the jar of plain water float on the surface, while the strings in the detergent water soon sink to the bottom.

WHY:

The strings that dropped to the bottom of the glass of detergent water had become water-soaked. The water and detergent mixture is an emulsion, or liquids floating in one another. This emulsion caused the strings to get wetter faster. The simple idea of using detergent as a "wetting agent" helps to remove dirt from clothes.

Keep these materials for the next experiment, **Clean As a Whistle**.

. . . .

Clean As a Whistle

Now let's really challenge detergent, using newly soiled strings.

You need:

more short strings

substances to soil strings;
  grease, oil, dirt, jam, juice, etc.

jars with water and detergent solution from Soapsud Derby (page 59)

spoon

WHAT TO DO:

Soil pairs of strings in juice, grease, dirt, oil, ketchup, mustard, or whatever you have on hand, and drop one of each pair into the jars. Stir the contents of each container. After ten minutes, remove the strings from the jars.

WHAT HAPPENS:

The strings in the detergent solution appear cleaner, while the strings in the glass of plain water do not.

WHY:

Again, the emulsifying effect of the detergent in the water thoroughly soaks the strings and easily lifts the dirt from them. This is seen by the now-discolored water in the detergent solution.

Take It to the Cleaners

Chemists are always working with new chemicals and trying to find out which ones clean best. Some everyday foods found around the kitchen make good cleaners, too, but which ones?

You need:

margarine, oil or butter
piece of white cotton cloth
$1/4$ lemon
paper towels

$1/4$ piece onion
vinegar
$1/2$ cup (120 mL) whole milk
marking pen

WHAT TO DO:

With the margarine, oil, or butter, make several grease marks, or stains, on the cloth. Make certain they are not too close

together. Take the cloth and spread it out on a hard kitchen surface. Squeeze some lemon juice onto a paper towel and, while holding the cloth against the hard surface, rub the juice on the towel against one of the marks. Rub hard and try to remove the stain. Crush the onion in another paper towel to make some juice and try to remove a second stain in the same way. Do the same with the vinegar and then the milk. Make certain you record on the cloth which substances you used to clean the different grease stains.

WHAT HAPPENS:

The lemon, onion, and vinegar remove stains a little, but not as well as the milk does.

WHY:

The milk does a better job of neutralizing, or canceling out, the stains. This is a case of "like will dissolve like." The butterfat in whole milk will dissolve grease stains such as that caused by fat in butter or margarine. Substances that have similar fat content will dissolve one another.

Put Out the Fire

Make your own fire extinguisher with a few materials you can find around your house.

You need:

large, wide-mouth jar with lid
large nail
hammer
2 cups (480 mL) water

3 tablespoons (45 mL) baking soda
spoon
small jar
$1/_2$ cup (120 mL) vinegar

WHAT TO DO:

First, on a rock outside or on an old workbench or board, turn the lid of the large jar over, and with the hammer and nail pound a large hole through it. *(Get adult help, if needed!)*

Pour the water into the large jar. Add the baking soda and mix. Fill the small jar with vinegar and gently place it, without a lid, into the large jar, making certain that the vinegar jar does not spill its contents. Screw the punctured lid onto the large jar, *making sure to hold it away from your face, and tip the jar toward the sink.*

WHAT HAPPENS:

A foamy liquid spurts out of the hole in the lid.

WHY:

Baking soda (sodium bicarbonate) puts out fires when used in soda-acid fire extinguishers. In your homemade version, the vinegar (acetic acid) mixes with the baking soda to produce the carbon dioxide (CO_2), a gas that smothers fires.

. . . .

Eggs-tra Bounce: All It Takes Is a Little Vinegar

Can an egg be changed chemically by placing it in different compounds?

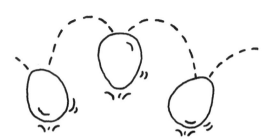

You need:

2 whole raw eggs (in shell)

glass of water

glass of vinegar

WHAT TO DO:

Put one egg in the glass of water and the other egg in the vinegar and let them stand for a full 24 hours.

WHAT HAPPENS:

The egg in the water remains the same, while the egg in the vinegar compound now feels and looks like a rubber ball, and no longer has a shell! If you drop it a short distance into the sink, it will actually bounce. Now you know how this experiment got its name.

WHY:

In the vinegar, a chemical change took place in the egg. The acetic acid (vinegar) reacted with the calcium carbonate of the eggshell. The change caused the shell to soften and then dissolve while the egg in the glass of water did not chemically change. Chemists would say that the shell of the egg in the vinegar became "decalcified."

No Bones About It!

Can you make chicken bones soft and even bend them? Try this experiment and see.

You need:
large wide-mouth jar
$1^1/_2$ cups of (360 mL) vinegar
some clean chicken bones (leg bones work best)

WHAT TO DO:
Put the vinegar into the jar and put the clean bones in it. Make certain the bones are completely covered by the vinegar. Leave the bones to set for two days.

WHAT HAPPENS:
The chicken bones are no longer hard, but soft.

WHY:
Bones are chiefly made up of the minerals calcium and phosphorus. When you soak the chicken bones in vinegar (acetic acid) a chemical change takes place and the mineral (stiffening) matter in them dissolves.

Water Softener

How would you like to make your own bath solution? This one will make your water softer, and soft water makes more suds to clean you better. It's fun and easy, and it's real chemistry.

You need:

$^1/_2$ cup (70 g) washing soda
saucer or small dish
spoon
clean, medium-size jar with lid, filled with water

WHAT TO DO:

Pour some of the washing soda into the saucer. With the back of the spoon, crush the crystals of washing soda into a fine powder. Spoon the washing soda powder into the jar of water a little at a time until no more will dissolve. (If needed, crush more washing soda powder and add it to the jar of water.) You now have a "saturated solution." Store the solution in the jar and add a small amount to the water when you take your bath.

WHAT HAPPENS:

The washing soda dissolves in the water and creates a natural bathwater softener.

WHY:

Sodium carbonate, or washing soda, neutralizes, or softens, water by removing hard bath salts, such as calcium. When this happens, chemists call it precipitation, but unlike weather forecasters, they don't mean rain, the soft water that falls from the sky. Here, precipitation is the chemical splitting of the two compounds calcium salts and washing soda into simpler molecules that form a solid substance called a precipitate. (See also **Presto-Perfect Precipitate,** page 79.)

Designer Bath Solution

Add special cologne, scents, or other ingredients, such as food coloring, to make your solution look and smell good. Put your special bath softener in fancy-shaped bottles or jars, and tie on some colorful ribbons. It makes a great and inexpensive homemade gift, and a little simple chemistry makes it all possible!

Shiny Silver Coins

Why not make your own silver cleaner? It's cheaper and may be better than cleaner from the store.

You need:

small container

1 teaspoon (5 mL) baking soda

1 teaspoon (5 mL) salt

water

silver coins

small enamel or glass pot

some aluminum foil

use of stove

soft cloth

WHAT TO DO:

In the small container, dissolve the salt and soda in a small amount of water. Place the coins in the water so that it covers them. Fill the small glass or enamel pot with water. Tear the aluminum foil into pieces and add them to the pot. Bring the water in the pot to a boil on the stove (you may want to ask a parent to assist you), then turn off the heat and let the water stand and cool. Remove the coins from the salt and soda solution. Rinse the coins in the cooled aluminum water, and dry them with a soft cloth.

WHAT HAPPENS:

You are now the proud owner of many shiny, sparkling-clean coins.

WHY:

Chemical reactions take place among the salt and soda (loosens tarnish) and the aluminum-foil solution. The heat turns the water and aluminum foil into an electrolyte solution, which carries a mild electric current that takes the tarnish off the coins.

Copperhead

Can you see whose head is on the penny or other dark, copper coins? If they are very dark and dull, it may be hard to tell. But it takes only a few minutes and a little simple chemistry to turn that dirty, dull copper into bright, shiny coins.

You need:

dark, dull copper coins
small, flat container
2 disposable cups
1 teaspoon (5 mL) salt

1 tablespoon (15 mL) water
2 tablespoons (30 mL) vinegar
medicine dropper
paper towel

WHAT TO DO:

Place the coins in the container. In one cup, make a solution with the salt and water. Pour the vinegar into the other cup. With the medicine dropper, drop the salt solution on the pennies, followed by the vinegar. Repeat these steps and keep the pennies in the solution for five minutes. Clean the pennies by wiping them off with a damp paper towel.

WHAT HAPPENS:

The pennies turn shiny-bright and the dark and dull film is removed.

WHY:

When combined with the salt (sodium chloride) the vinegar (acetic acid) chemically changes into a weak solution of hydrochloric acid. Hydrochloric acid cleans metals like copper. After a while, the pennies will oxidize, or become dull and dark, again because of the water and oxygen molecules that they come in contact with in the air.

Oxidation: Rust Race

When one substance gives oxygen to another, chemists say it is "reduced," and the substance that receives the oxygen is said to be "oxidized." Confused?

Think of it this way: You have ten balls that stand for oxygen and a friend takes seven of them. Your friend would be oxidized, because he received extra oxygen from you, but you would be reduced because you lost some of your oxygen. Now you can produce this chemical change, oxidation, and see how it works.

You need:

metal objects: paper clips, nails, washers, steel wool, tacks, pins
jars with lids: of various sizes
liquids: water, salt solution, vinegar

WHAT TO DO:

Place a selection of metal objects into the various jars. Add two tablespoons of one of the liquids to each jar. Screw lids tightly on some jars; leave the other jars without lids. Place some of your experiments in shady, cool places, others in warm, sunny places. Set the experiments aside for one to three weeks. Keep good records: dates and times you started the experiments, substances used, and see what happens.

WHAT HAPPENS:

A reddish-brown or brownish-yellow substance forms on some of the metal object, but maybe not on all.

WHY:

Moisture, an oxidizing agent, causes oxygen from the air to attach to certain metals, like iron and steel, to form rust. This chemical change, called oxidation, corrodes, or rots metal. That is why bridges and fire escapes, which often get wet, must be painted to protect them from being rotted and weakened by oxidation.

WHAT NOW:

Did some objects rust while others didn't? Try to figure out why. Maybe the oxidation takes a longer time, or the object is protected by a coating of non-rusting material. Redo the experiments exactly, or change one of the variables, and see what happens then. Compare the results.

The Gas Guzzler

A car is called a gas guzzler when it uses a lot of gas. In this experiment, gas wastes water. Try it and see!

You need:

a 4 x 4 piece of coffee filter

3 teaspoons (15 mL) baking soda
  (sodium bicarbonate)

rubber band

tall narrow jar filled with water

a shallow bowl of water

permanent marker

magnifying glass

WHAT TO DO:

Place the baking soda in the middle of the filter. Gather the filter together to make a pouch and fasten the top with a rubber band. Place the baking soda pouch in the tall jar of water and place your hand over the opening. With your hands in place on the bottom and the top of the jar, turn the jar upside down and place its opening in the bowl of water. Remove your hands. Mark the water line on the jar. Watch the glass jar with the magnifying lens. Be patient; you must wait at least an hour for results.

WHAT HAPPENS:

Bubbles rise from the pouch in the bottom of the jar to the top of it. Some bubbles cling to the sides of the jar. Within an hour, the water drops slightly, but noticeably, below the marked water line.

WHY:

As the baking soda in the pouch is dissolved by the water, it produces carbon dioxide gas (CO_2) this gas needs room in the jar so it displaces the water, or forces some of it out of the jar, lowering the water level.

. . . .

King Kong's Hand

King Kong's hand must have been very big to hold a lady in it. Now, you can make your own big hand with just a few simple materials. Without the marker lines, the hand becomes a cow's udder, the bag under the cow that holds its milk—an udderly fantastic trick! Anyway you look at it, it's pure chemistry and it will teach you about an important gas that all chemists know.

You need:

disposable latex glove (available in packages of ten)

brown or black permanent marker (optional)

$1/4$ cup (35 g) baking soda

$1/2$ cup (120 mL) vinegar

NOTE: A friend or assistant would be helpful for this experiment, and it's best done over a sink or basin (or outside) as it can be messy!

WHAT TO DO:

For a King Kong hand, make short vertical lines with the marker pen on each side of the glove to represent King Kong's hairy hand. If you're making a cow's udder, leave the glove plain.

Have your helper hold the glove over the sink or basic while you pour the baking soda, followed by the vinegar, into the glove. Now, very quickly, close the opening of the glove with your hand to make an airtight seal. Hold it tightly for several minutes.

WHAT HAPPENS:

The glove blows up like a balloon—then, after another few minutes, goes back to its normal size.

WHY:

When you mixed the baking soda and vinegar together, you made a very popular gas called carbon dioxide (CO_2). This is why the solution started to fizz and foam and spill out over the top of the glove before you closed it up. Once the gas is trapped in the glove, it has no place to go, so it blows the glove up. Eventually, the reaction dies down, the gas succeeds in escaping, and the glove returns to its normal size.

What a Gas!

Baking soda (sodium bicarbonate) is a compound made up of the elements hydrogen, sodium, oxygen, and carbon. When vinegar is added (water and acetic acid), a chemical reaction takes place; the elements carbon and oxygen link together to make a new gaseous compound called carbon dioxide. (For more carbon dioxide experiments, see **The Lab: CO_2 and You!**, page 117.)

Exothermic Exercise

What kind of chemical change takes place when yeast mixes with hydrogen peroxide? This extremely exciting experiment is bound to warm you up.

You need:

thermometer

pencil and paper

small bowl

$1/4$ cup (60 mL) hydrogen peroxide

1 teaspoon (5 mL) quick-rising dry yeast

spoon

WHAT TO DO:

Record the temperature showing on the thermometer, and then place it in the bowl. Pour in the hydrogen peroxide, add the yeast, and stir the solution. As you watch what happens, feel the lower sides and bottom of the bowl. Wait a minute or two; then spoon out the thermometer and record the temperature again.

WHAT HAPPENS:

The solution foams and bubbles, and the bottom and sides of the bowl feel very warm. Steam can be seen coming from the solution. The higher thermometer reading shows that heat has been produced.

WHY:

When yeast and hydrogen peroxide mix chemically, the hydrogen peroxide change into oxygen and water molecules. The bubbles are produced by the oxygen gas escaping during the chemical change. This change also produces heat. When heat is produced in a chemical change, we call the process exothermic.

Endothermic Cold Wave

If a chemical change can cause heat (exothermic), can another chemical change make something cold?

You need:

medium-size jar

tap water, neither hot nor cold

thermometer

1 tablespoon (15mL) Epsom salts

pencil and paper

WHAT TO DO:

Fill the jar with tap water. Place the thermometer in the water. With your hand, feel the coolness of the jar while you wait until

the thermometer registers the water's temperature. Write the temperature down. Now stir in the Epsom salts. Feel the jar again. Is there a change? After a couple of minutes, take out the thermometer and record the temperature again.

WHAT HAPPENS:

The jar feels slightly colder, and the temperature of the water after the chemical change is actually lower.

WHY:

In the previous experiment, **Exothermic Exercise**, a chemical change produced heat energy. But sometimes heat is instead used up in the chemical change. When Epsom salts, or magnesium sulfate, is added to water, it uses the water's natural heat energy to split apart ions of sulfate and magnesium. (Ions are positive or negative electrically charged atoms that occur when electrons are lost or gained.) The chemical change in this experiment is called endothermic because more heat energy is being used up than is being produced. This is why the water gets colder and why Epsom salts are used to soak a sprained ankle and draw the heat out of an injury.

. . . .

Marvelous Marbling

Wrap small presents up in your homemade marble-colored gift wrap. When dried, this paper is like parchment, a crisp, crinkly, see-through kind of paper. It's crispy, it's streaky—it's simply *marbelous*!

You need:

newspaper

a large bowl or basin
  (plastic or rubber is best)

2 tablespoons (30 mL) vinegar

paper towels or napkins

small pieces of colored chalk*

hammer or heavy stone
  (for crushing chalk)

2 to 6 disposable cups*

cooking oil

a disposable plastic spoon or fork

half sheets of white typing paper*

*Quantities depend on how many colors and how much colored paper you want.

WHAT TO DO:

Place some newspaper over the kitchen counter. Fill the bowl to the top with water and add the vinegar. Place the bowl in the middle of the newspaper. Put down extra newspaper for drying papers after you've colored them. Place several doubled paper towels on top of the newspaper and set a different-colored piece of chalk in the center of each. Crush the chalk to a fine powder.

Carefully lifting the towels, put the powdered chalk into as many disposable cups as you have colors. Place a tablespoon of oil into each cup, stirring thoroughly with the plastic fork or spoon. Pour the contents of each cup into the bowl of water. The chalky oil should form large colored circular pools on the surface of the water. Now, carefully, lay each piece of paper on the surface of the water and lift off.

Dry the colored papers on newspaper over the next 24 hours. When they are fully dried, gently wipe off any surface chalk grains with a paper towel.

WHAT HAPPENS:

The colored oil sticks to the paper and makes circles and streaky patterns.

WHY:

Negative- and positive-charged molecules are attracted to one another. The molecules of chalk (a type of calcium carbonate) and vinegar (acetic acid) and water and the surface of the paper all chemically combine to cause a chemical bond that causes the swirling colors to stick to the paper.

Presto-Perfect Precipitate ☠

I bet you can't say that fast ten times! You can, however, make a precipitate in just seconds. If you remember, a precipitate is a substance that forms when a chemical reaction or change occurs. This substance is also insoluble. That means it does not dissolve or evenly mix as does a substance in a solution.

You need:
a small jar half-filled with water
1 teaspoon (5 mL) Epsom salts
window cleaner with ammonia
1 teaspoon (5 mL) alum

WHAT TO DO:
Dissolve the Epsom salts in the jar and add a few squirts of window cleaner.

WHAT HAPPENS:
The solution becomes milky white.

WHY:
When magnesium sulfate (Epsom salts) is mixed with ammonium hydroxide (ammonia solution), it forms a new chemical compound. The milky white liquid formed is a precipitate of magnesium hydroxide. *(Be careful when disposing of this solution.)*

WHAT NOW:
Repeat the same activity but now use alum (found in the spice section of the supermarket) instead of the Epsom salts. You'll make a new precipitate called aluminum hydroxide. Compare the color change of the magnesium hydroxide with that of the aluminum hydroxide.

SALTY SOLUTIONS AND SWEET SUCCESS

Without salt and sugar, life would be very dull. Most important, we could not live without a proper balance of sugar and salt in our bodies. Now, we'll find out just what these chemical compounds are all about and what they can do.

Salt and Sugar

Salt (NaCl) is a mineral compound, which in this case means it is a combination of two elements and is a crystal substance. Each salt crystal is made up of millions of atoms that fasten on to one another. Salt is made up of the elements sodium and chlorine (a compound). Sodium is a metal solid and chlorine is a greenish gas. By themselves, these two chemicals are extremely dangerous but when they are combined into a compound, they become common table salt.

Sugar is a carbohydrate, or a chemical compound made up of carbon, hydrogen, and oxygen. Common table sugar is called sucrose. Other sugars are glucose, fructose, lactose, and maltose.

The Sugar Cube Race

Will more sugar cubes dissolve, or disappear, in cold water than in hot or warm tap water? Let's have a race and find out.

You need:
sugar cubes

clear glass of very hot tap water

clear glass of cold tap water

paper and pencil

spoon

WHAT TO DO:
Put a cube of sugar in the cold water and stir until its crystals disappear, or dissolve, completely. Continue to put sugar cubes

into the water one at a time—count them—until no more sugar will dissolve. You'll know when this happens, because the crystal grains of sugar will begin to show in the solution and will start to gather on the bottom of the glass.

Now, repeat this activity using hot water. Make certain you count the number of cubes that dissolve in each glass of water. Record, or write, the number for each. Which can hold the most dissolved sugar cubes?

WHAT HAPPENS:

Fewer cubes should dissolve thoroughly in the cold tap water than in the hot.

WHY:

The first sugar cubes dissolve in each glass of water until no more sugar crystals can be seen. Then, as more cubes are added, the solutions reach a point where the crystals can no longer disappear and they can easily be seen. Scientists and chemists call this a saturated solution. More sugar dissolves in the hot water than in the cold because, when water is heated, its molecules move faster and farther apart. As a result, the spaces between the water molecules become larger, allowing room for more sugar molecules.

Sweet and Slow

Which dissolves faster, a whole sugar cube or a crushed one?

You need:

newspaper

2 sugar cubes

small disposable container

heavy spoon

2 glasses half-filled with water

WHAT TO DO:

Set out a thick layer of newspaper and place the container onto it. Using the back of the spoon, crush one of the cubes in the container. (Ask an adult to help you if you're not strong enough.) Put each in its separate glass of water at the same time.

WHAT HAPPENS:

The crushed sugar cube dissolves faster.

WHY:

The water molecules must dissolve all of the outside parts of the solid sugar cube before they can reach and dissolve the inside. This takes longer. Because the water molecules come in contact with more outside surfaces when the sugar cube is crushed, the rate of solubility (or how fast a substance dissolves) is quicker.

Sweet Talk

Our bodies are complicated chemical factories, as this simple experiment shows.

You need:
unsalted soda crackers

WHAT TO DO:
Chew a soda cracker slowly for a few minutes.

WHAT HAPPENS:
The cracker tastes sweet.

WHY:
Your saliva has a substance in it called an enzyme. The enzyme styalin breaks down starch or other carbohydrate molecules to a simple sugar called maltose. When you chew the cracker, the starch in it is changed to sugar, so it tastes sweet.

Carbohydrates

The organic compounds called carbohydrates are found in foods such as sugar, bread, potatoes, and crackers. They are made up of carbon, hydrogen, and oxygen atoms.

Sweet Tooth

Want to see how fast a tooth dissolves in a cola drink. Don't pull out a tooth for this experiment, but if you happen to have an extra tooth lying around the house, try it!

You need:
tooth
glass of cola drink (regular)

WHAT TO DO:
Place the tooth in the cola beverage. Leave it in the drink for at least a week.

WHAT HAPPENS:
The tooth starts to dissolve.

WHY:
Now you know why your parents and dentists warn you about drinking too many sugary drinks with a high acid content. Even though your teeth wouldn't be constantly sitting in a cola drink, the high sugar and acid content of these drinks can chemically affect your teeth over time. In this experiment, the sugar and acid eventually cause the tooth to dissolve, right through its hard enamel surface coating.

Wash Out the Salt!

You can remove ice from the streets in winter by using salt, but can you remove salt from ice?

In **The Water Factory** (page 26) we boiled water and left salt behind, but now we'll wash it out and shake the habit for good!

You need:

jar large enough to hold
  2 cups (480 mL) cold water

1 teaspoon (5 mL) salt

spoon

6 disposable cups

freezer

marking pen

a coffee filter

ice

WHAT TO DO:

In the jar, dissolve the salt in the water and stir with a spoon. Pour some of the salt water solution into one of the cups ($^3/_4$ filled) and place it in the freezer. It will take about two hours for the ice to get slushy.

Save the rest of the salt water in the jar. Later, we'll compare this water, called a "control," with our desalted or no-salt water.

While waiting for the water to freeze, number the five remaining cups: 1, 2, 3, 4, 5 with the marker. Write "salted" on cup number 1, and "desalted" on cup number 5. When the two hours are almost up, fill cups 2, 3, and 4 about $^3/_4$ full with ice water (put a few ice cubes in each cup).

The next steps must be done carefully but quickly, before the slushy ice melts. Place the slushy ice from the cup in the freezer (a small clump will be in the bottom) into the coffee filter. Twist the filter to make a pouch and quickly dip it, three times, into each of the three cups of ice water in turn. Transfer what's left of the ice to the cup marked desalted. Pour an equal amount of salt water from the jar (the "control") into cup number 1, marked salted. Now, dip a finger into each of these two cups and taste the difference.

WHAT HAPPENS:

The water that was "washed" tastes less salty. Put all the cups aside and let the water evaporate. Which cup has the most salt crystals? Which has the least?

WHY:

As the water froze, the salt that was dissolved in it was forced to the surface of the ice, where it was washed off. Now you know two ways to separate salt and water. In distillation, you boiled the water away and left the salt behind, but here you took the salt out of the water and left the liquid behind.

Try doing this same experiment with seawater. Do you think this method would be a good way to provide fresh, cheap drinking water?

Watercooler

Which is colder, regular ice water or salted ice water?

You need:

marking pen

2 disposable cups

2 thermometers

10 ice cubes

1 tablespoon (15 mL) salt

paper and pencil

WHAT TO DO:

With the marker, label one cup "salt" and the other "no salt." Place a thermometer in each cup. Pack the ice cubes around the thermometers, five cubes to each cup. Pour the salt over and between the ice cubs in one cup. Wait about thirty minutes for results. Read the temperature on each thermometer and write it down.

WHAT HAPPENS:

The temperature in the cup with the salted ice water is colder.

WHY:

Water freezes at 32 degrees Fahrenheit, or 0 degrees centigrade. In the unsalted water, the temperature is usually above freezing, while the salted water is much below. The salt draws heat from the ice and makes it much colder while lowering the freezing point on the thermometer.

WHAT NOW:

Do this same experiment again, but this time substitute crushed ice (see **I've Got a Crush on You**, page 91) for ice cubes. Does crushed ice make the water colder. Write down the temperature reading in each experiment and compare the differences, if any.

Ice Show

Will ice cubes stick together better with salt, or with no salt?

You need:

12 ice cubes
1 teaspoon (5 mL) salt
paper and pencil

WHAT TO DO:

Place three ice cubes on top of three others. Mark these "no salt." Take three more cubes, sprinkle a little salt on top of each, and place the last three cubes on top of the salted cubes. Mark these "with salt." Wait about five minutes until all the cubes are partially melted.

WHAT HAPPENS:

The salted ice cubes stick together better than the unsalted cubes.

WHY:

The water molecules move from one cube to the next while attaching themselves together. Both sets of ice cubes stick, but the cubes with the salt stick better. The salt makes the ice melt more rapidly, so the molecules move from one cube to another and attach themselves faster. This is why salt is used on roads on winter days.

Ice Bound

If you're surrounded by ice, you're bound to freeze. In this experiment, you can make water freeze to a solid state in about thirty minutes, and you won't have to use the refrigerator freezer!

You need:

olive jar or other narrow jar
small bowl of crushed ice
dish towels or paper towels

$^1/_4$ cup (48 g) salt
thermometer
paper and pencil

WHAT TO DO:

Fill the narrow jar one-quarter full with water and place it in the middle of the bowl. Pack the crushed ice around the jar in the bowl. Fold enough paper towels or dish towels to cover the outside of the bowl and set it against a stable object to keep the towels in place. Place the thermometer in the narrow jar and write down the starting temperature. Pour the salt onto the crushed ice and work it in. After about thirty minutes, record the temperature again. If the water is not yet frozen, wait until the temperature reaches 32°F (0°C) or below.

WHAT HAPPENS:
The water turns to a solid state (ice) or at least a partly solid state (ice crystals, slush).

WHY:
When salt is placed on the ice, heat is taken from the bottle and the water's temperature is lowered below the freezing point.

I've Got a Crush on You

If your refrigerator does not have a crushed ice dispenser, ice cubes can be crushed in a special appliance, food processor, or blender, or by putting them in a towel and breaking them up with a hammer.

In an electric blender, place 2 cups (400 g) of ice cubes into the blender container, along with one cup (240 mL) of water. Press the CHOP or high-speed button to blend. Turn off the blender occasionally, and stir the ice with a rubber spatula or wooden spoon. This will distribute the cubes equally so that they can be crushed more evenly.

If needed, ask for help making crushed ice.

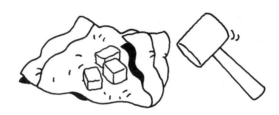

IT'S CRYSTAL CLEAR

Crystals are everywhere. Snow, sugar, salt, parts of rocks, and precious jewels are all crystals. Crystals are made up of atoms that join together in a certain way.

In this part of the book, you'll make crystals from table and rock salt, bluing, sugar, washing soda, and alum. When you're finished, you can invite your friends over for a gem show and display all the crystals you've grown.

Your Diamond Ring? Just Another Carbon Copy!

Diamonds are carbon crystals. Carbon, as you remember, is an element. Volcanos are nature's chemists. The heat and pressure of volcanos crystallized the carbon into diamonds. When lava reaches the surface of the earth, it cools and hardens and forms a rock called kimberlite. Diamonds are found in kimberlite. Tons of kimberlite have to be washed and crushed just to find one small diamond.

The diamond is the hardest substance found on earth. An imperfect diamond, one not good enough to be mounted on a ring, makes a perfect tool for cutting hard metals. Diamonds are so hard they can cut anything. (If you find something you think might be a diamond, test it by trying to cut with it. If it doesn't cut, it is probably only a piece of glass.)

Sparkling Soda

No, we're not using soda pop in this experiment, but washing soda. That's right! Although this soda is all washed up in this activity, it still sparkles!

You need:
disposable cup half-filled with hot tap water   spoon
$1/_2$ cup (120 mL) washing soda   magnifying glass

WHAT TO DO:
Pour the washing soda slowly into the water, stirring as you

pour, until no more will dissolve. Set the cup aside and check the experiment often over the next few hours.

WHAT HAPPENS:

As the water cools and begins to evaporate, crystals form on the sides and bottom of the cup.

WHY:

When you dissolve the washing soda (solute) into the hot water (solvent) until no more can be dissolved, you put more solute in the water than it can possibly hold when it is cool. When this saturated solution cools, the washing soda molecules hook up with each other and form crystals.

WHAT NOW:

Pour the washing soda crystals from the cup into a shallow disposable container such as a frozen food tray. Place them in a warm, sunny place for 24 hours and let the water evaporate. (See **Astronomical White Asteroids**, below.)

Astronomical White Asteroids

Asteroids are irregularly shaped, rocklike chunks in space. Like the planets, they revolve around the sun. Your washing soda, after it is chemically changed, will look very much like these rocklike chunks of space matter. The different-size crystals can be compared to the different-size asteroids, the smallest being less than one mile wide, the largest about 500 miles wide. Save these Sparkling Soda asteroid chunks for **The Gem Show**, page 101, and use this information for one of your labels.

Chemistry in a Cave

Most caves are made of limestone. Limestone is a rock that can be easily worn away by water. Over thousands of years, this solution of water and calcium bicarbonate has gradually carved out great rooms in huge pieces of rock. This same solution drips though cracks in cave ceilings. As the water evaporates in the air, carbon dioxide is given off and the solid mineral calcite is formed. This turns into the hard lime icicle deposits, known as stalactites, found hanging from cave ceilings. Stalagmites are similar shaped rock formations that build up on the floor, because of the dripping, instead of on the ceiling.

Crazy Cave Icicles

You can make your own crystal rock formations (stalagmite and stalactites) to demonstrate how chemistry in a cave really works.

You need:

2 one-pint (480 mL) jars
hot tap water
1 cup (240 mL) washing soda

dishcloth
3 small pieces of string
small dish

WHAT TO DO:

Fill the two jars almost to the top with hot tap water. Stir washing soda into each jar until no more will dissolve. Twist the dishcloth and tie the ends and the middle with the strings. Place the ends of the "rope" you have made into the two jars of water, forming a bridge. Make certain that the rope ends touch the bottoms of the jars. Place the dish under the cloth bridge to collect the drips. Allow 3 to 5 days for "icicles" to form.

WHAT HAPPENS:

The water and soda solution travels up both sides of the dishcloth rope and drips from the middle. The drips turn into hard soda pillars with the two columns meeting in the middle. Something similar happens in caves. However, the buildup of cave deposits takes hundreds of years, while yours take only a few days.

WHY:

The water travels through the dishcloth rope by filling up all the tiny air pockets in the cloth. This is known as capillary action and it is similar to a row of dominoes falling down. (See **Fluttering Flatworm Marathon**, page 35) The washing soda is carried along the "rope" by the water, which drips down from the middle. The water evaporates and leaves behind the hardened soda pillar. When you stir the washing soda into the jars until no more can be dissolved, you saturate it. The cooled solution's molecules then crystallize, or harden.

About Crystals

Crystals can be grown from a string tied to a pencil and placed across a cup or glass, or scraped with a spoon from the sides and bottom of the container. Keep the crystal solution in a warm, sunny window. The longer the crystal solution is left to evaporate, the larger the crystals will be.

Store your crystals in a dry place and be careful handling them. If your hands are wet or damp, it is best to use tweezers or a plastic spoon.

Blue Moon Rocks

You'll think you've stepped out on the moon when you grow this crystal garden. Make certain you cover your work area with newspapers so you don't have crystals growing everywhere!

You need:

frozen-food tray
paper towels
a disposable cup
3 tablespoons (45 mL) salt
3 tablespoons (45 mL) water

3 tablespoons (45 mL)
  laundry bluing
spoon
magnifying glass

WHAT TO DO:

Place a folded paper towel in the bottom of the tray. Crush another second paper towel and place it on top. In the disposable cup, mix together the salt, water, and bluing and slowly spoon the mixture over the paper. Observe what happens using the magnifying lens.

WHAT HAPPENS:

Blue bubbly crystals instantly appear in the container. (For a full garden, it will have to set for at least 24 hours.)

WHY:

The salt solution with the bluing becomes saturated until no more can dissolve. As the water is soaked up by the paper towels and evaporates, the salt left behind forms new crystals around the powdery bluing.

Rocky Mountains

Watch these beautiful rock salt crystals climb on the sides of a string and turn into sparkling mountains of diamondlike cubes. Follow the instructions as in **The Diamond Mine** (page 99) but replace the alum with $1/_4$ cup (48g) of rock salt. Use a strong string dangling from a pencil to catch the growing crystals. Don't rush this one! Great mountains of crystals may take as long as two to four weeks to grow.

The Diamond Mine

Alum is a type of mineral or chemical salt that puts the pucker into some pickles, making your mouth feel as if it wants to close up. It looks and feels very much like table salt (sodium chloride), but while table salt under a microscope looks like ice cubes, with flat sides, alum crystals have many angular sides, or facets. Try making your own clear alum crystals and you'll think you've discovered a diamond mine.

You need:

small bottle of alum
(available in the supermarket)

disposable cup half-filled
with warm water

spoon

small jar

piece of nylon thread

pencil

magnifying glass

WHAT TO DO:

Slowly and carefully pour the alum into the cup of water, stirring as you pour, until no more will dissolve. You'll know when the solution is saturated because you'll hear the alum grains scratching on the bottom of the cup and you'll see some floating in the water. If you put your finger in the cup and touch the bottom, you'll be able to feel the undissolved crystals. Keep the solution in the cup overnight.

The next day, pour the water into the jar and tie one end of the nylon thread around a large piece of hardened alum crystal you'll find in the bottom or on the sides of the cup. (Be patient with this. If you've ever threaded a sewing needle, you'll understand what we mean. It's hard to tie the fine nylon thread around the small alum crystals.) Wind and tie the other end of the thread around the middle of a pencil and place the pencil over the jar mouth so that the alum dangles low in the water. Keep the jar in a protected place for several days and observe the crystals from time to time.

NOTE: Save the other alum crystals on the bottom of the paper cup and set them to dry on a paper towel. Place them on a dark piece of construction paper and study them with your magnifying lens. Save these shiny, many-sided alum crystals for The Gem Show, page 101.

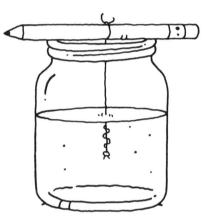

WHAT HAPPENS:

If you hold the thread up to the light and view the alum crystals, you'll see what appears to be many shiny brilliant gems.

WHY:

Again the crystals are formed by dissolving enough solutes or solid substances (in this case alum) in the water (solvent) to make a saturated solution. Then the cooled solution causes the alum molecules on the string to build on one another. Crystals will continue to form on the crystal string until all of the solution evaporates.

Hi Sugar!

With all your experience with saturated solutions, now make a saturated sugar solution. You can use a string on a pencil to catch your crystals or leave them in the bottom of a jar or cup and collect them later. Keep them for displaying in **The Gem Show** (below).

Unlike salt crystals, which look like cubes, sugar crystals are long and have flat, slanted sides.

. . . .

The Gem Show

Invite your friends over for a gem show. It's easy and it's lots of fun! Display your sugar, salt, alum, and washing soda crystals in a special way. Line lids of small boxes with dark paper or cloth and place your crystals in them. Place the lids on an outside table for "crystal viewing" on a sunny day. Use information from this book to make labels for your crystal trays. Supply plenty of magnifying glasses for viewing. You can even give a demonstration on how to make crystals with a saturated solution.

Also, you can separate your crystals and glue some onto rings for a special display. (Plain rings can be purchased at hobby stores or made with pipe cleaners.) Try adding a drop or two of food coloring to your solutions when you make crystals. You'll be able to make simulated, or fake, rubies, emeralds, and sapphires. You can add these to your rings, make crystal-designed holiday ornaments, or use them in other crafts. With a little imagination, the possibilities for exciting crystal-craft projects are endless.

KITCHEN ALCHEMY

Most people don't think of cooking as chemistry, but when batters turn into cakes, cookies, and pancakes, and sugar crystallizes and turns into candy, it definitely is.

In fact, most cooking does involve chemical change or reactions. Carbon dioxide gas, through yeast, makes bread rise, and salt causes water to leave pickles through a process called osmosis.

Don't be too surprised if these experiment-recipes become family favorites. Besides being great chemistry experiments and fun to make, they're fantastically delicious!

Spicy Infusion

Chemists often use the word *infusion*. Anything dissolved in hot water is called an infusion. Some people drink infusions every day in the form of coffee and tea. In this activity, you'll make your own infusions and you'll have the fun of drinking them, too!

You need:
teakettle with boiling water

small kitchen strainer or a tea ball

$1/_2$ teaspoon (2 mL) each of at least 6 herbs or spices:
whole parts, such as a bay leaf or the leaves of oregano,
basil, mint, or parsley; buds or seeds, such as cloves,
mustard, fennel, or anise,or bark, such as cinnamon
or sassafras.

teacups or mugs

spoons

paper and pencil to
record solubility and tastes

WHAT TO DO:

Put one herb or spice in the strainer and place it on the top of a cup. Pour some water from the teakettle over it. Let the substances steep, or soak, for 2 to 3 minutes. Remove the strainer and clean it out under cold water. Now sip your infusion "tea" and describe its taste. Repeat these steps with the other herbs and spices.

WHAT HAPPENS:

The spices and herbs steep and dissolve in the water to color and flavor it.

WHY:

Some herbs and spicy substances are more soluble, or dissolve more easily, in hot water, than others. The chemical composition, or the way the molecules are arranged, has a lot to do with a substance's solubility. A tea may be sweet and pleasant, or bitter and sour. It may make your mouth pucker when you taste it, or may be so weak you can hardly taste it at all. What do you like or dislike about your infusions?

Host An Infusion Party

Invite some of your friends over on a wet and cold day for an infusion-test "tea" party. Provide a list of spices and herbs used but don't identify, or name, the samples. Have among your teas some made from such popular and favorite herbs and spices as nutmeg, anise seed, mint, fennel seed, allspice, cinnamon bark, and clove. Also try thin slices of ginger root. Use sugar or honey for flavoring and supply small disposable plastic spoons and cups for sampling. Serve your infusion teas with some light, crispy cookies. Give each person a pencil and a small notepad and ask them to identify each infusion and its solubility, or how well-flavored it is. Have fun and enjoy!

Taste, Bud?

How your tea tastes to you depends largely on your tongue. It has about 3,000 taste buds located on its surface. The taste buds on the sides react to sour substances, while those at the back react to bitterness. The taste buds toward the front of the tongue, especially, are sensitive to sweet and to salty tastes.

Interestingly, your sense of smell plays a big part in tasting food. Without this important sense, as when you have a bad head cold, you cannot even recognize the flavor of foods you are eating; you just can't "taste" anything.

Butter Me Up

You can make your own butter very easily. This experiment-recipe is made in small quantities to use immediately. It may take about ten minutes for your cream to turn to butter but it's definitely worth it—you *butter* believe it!

You need:
1 cup (240 mL) cold heavy whipping cream
small bowl chilled in refrigerator
electric hand mixer
measuring cup

WHAT TO DO:
Pour the cream into the chilled bowl. Mix on high until the cream forms yellow clumps. This will not happen right away; allow at least ten minutes. As you mix, a liquid separates from

the clumps. Pour this liquid off into the measuring cup as you continue to mix.

WHAT HAPPENS:
The cream is turned into butter, and there's a good bit of liquid in the measuring cup.

WHY:
Cream is a combination of butterfat and water molecules. The butterfat floats throughout the water. This, again, is an example of a suspension, a solid suspended in a liquid. When you use the mixer on the cream, the molecules of butterfat collide and stick together, the clumps get larger, and you have butter, a solid substance. The water molecule part of the cream is the liquid you now have in the measuring cup. How much of the cup of cream was butterfat and how much water?

. . . .

"Emulsional" About Mayonnaise

Don't cry over cracked eggs and when your egg whites get beaten up, send in the substitute! Whichever you use—egg whites or substitute—you can make mayonnaise in small quantities to use immediately. This serves 2 to 4.

You need:

small mixing bowl

2 tablespoons (30 mL) egg substitute

$1/2$ teaspoon (2 mL) mustard

1 teaspoon (5 mL) lemon juice

salt and pepper to taste

spoon for mixing

$1/2$ cup (120 mL) cooking oil

1 teaspoon (5 mL) boiling water

WHAT TO DO:

Place the egg substitute in the bowl. Add the mustard, lemon juice, and seasoning. Beat these with the spoon. Add the oil a little at a time, then beat. Add some more oil, and beat again. Do this until the mayonnaise gets stiff, then you can add the oil faster.

If the oil just seems to sit there (now you'll learn how emulsions act), simply add a touch more mustard and continue beating. The secret of making good mayonnaise is to keep on beating the ingredients. At the end, add a teaspoon (5 mL) of boiling water to keep your mayonnaise from separating.

WHAT HAPPENS:

From the separate ingredients, you have made mayonnaise, a mixture of liquids suspended or floating in one another, called an emulsion.

WHY:

In the case of mayonnaise, the mustard and the boiling water are the emulsifying agents that keep the oil and the lemon juice from separating and keep the mixture emulsified. Without these agents, the mixture can and will separate.

Tarragon Mayonnaise Dressing

Add shredded leaves of fresh tarragon (an herb found in your supermarket's produce department) to your mayonnaise, and you have a delicious, light salad dressing. It's great on sliced tomatoes, too!

In a Pickle

Now make some simple delicious pickles you can eat tonight. You'll be using salt and vinegar, compounds that keep foods from spoiling.

You need:

large unpeeled cucumber
fork
sharp knife
deep bowl
1 tablespoon (15 mL) salt
spoon

small plate and something to weigh it down, such as a can of soup
a small, covered serving container
1 tablespoon (15 mL) sugar
$3/4$ cup (180 mL) cider or white vinegar
parsley, or tarragon (fresh or dried)

WHAT TO DO:

Scrub the cucumber. With the help of an adult, cut deep grooves down and around the length of it with the prongs of a fork. Slice the cucumber thinly, so you can almost see through the slices. Place the slices in a deep bowl and sprinkle the salt on top. Toss the slices thoroughly with a spoon to mix in the salt. Cover the slices with a small plate and place something heavy on top. Let the cucumbers stand at room temperature for one hour.

Drain the slices and put them in the serving container. Mix the sugar and vinegar, and pour it over the cucumber slices. Chill thoroughly for two to three hours. Before serving, drain off the liquid and sprinkle with chopped parsley, dill, or tarragon. Enjoy!

WHAT HAPPENS:

The cucumbers turn into a simple version of crispy, crunchy pickle slices.

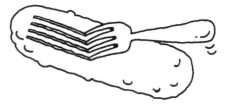

WHY:

The salt and vinegar combine to ferment the cucumber. The process, called osmosis, draws water out of the cucumbers to make the pickles crisp and crunchy.

Fermentation

Salt keeps foods from spoiling. Pickles are usually made by placing vegetables, usually cucumbers, in salt water. The salty solution is called a brine. The salt draws out the juices and helps the good bacteria change, or ferment, the cucumbers into pickles while killing the bad bacteria. Chemists know that bacteria are everywhere, even in our bodies. Some cause disease, while others cause chemical changes in foods to make new ones, such as pickles.

Lemon Aide

Chemistry, as you can see, is everywhere in the kitchen. Like candy, syrups are super-saturated solutions of sugar and water, and the difference between the two is the degree of heat that chemically changes the substances. In this recipe-experiment, you'll make your very own lemon syrup for instant fresh lemonade.

You need:

a pot	use of stove	a strainer
2 cups (380 g) sugar	1 cup (240 mL) lemon juice	a large clean jar or covered container
1 cup (240 mL) water		

WHAT TO DO:

Place the sugar and water in a pot. Boil the solution for five minutes; then let it cool and add the lemon juice. Pour the syrup through a strainer and into the container.

For keeping, store in the refrigerator. You'll need 2 tablespoons (30 mL) of syrup to one glass of ice water for a great fresh lemonade. Enjoy!

WHAT HAPPENS:

The sugar, lemon and water solution turns into a thick, lemony syrup.

WHY:

The heat causes the sugar and water to mix thoroughly, then it boils away some of the water molecules through steam, or water vapor. When the thickened sugar solution cools, it chemically reacts with the lemon juice, making the syrupy mixture.

. . . .

Atom's Apple

Try rearranging an apple's atoms, and make a delicious warm dessert that serves four.

You need:

large pot

$1^{1}/_{2}$ cups (350 mL) water

$^{1}/_{2}$ cup (95 g) sugar

lemon slice

6 small-medium apples

peeler and knife

use of stove

cinnamon

WHAT TO DO:

In the pot, cook the first three ingredients together for five minutes, then remove the lemon. With the help of an adult, peel, core, and slice the apples, and add them to the sugar solution, a few at a time. Cook until soft, adding water as needed.

To serve, set the apples to plates, pour warm sugar syrup over them and sprinkle with cinnamon.

WHAT HAPPENS:

The firm apples soften and make a delicious apple dessert.

WHY:

The lemon acid and sugar combine with a substance in the apples called pectin. This softens them into a jellylike mixture. The heated water helps break down the atoms of the apple or the structure of its molecules. Then it is chemically changed by "cooking," from a hard state to a soft one.

. . . .

Herb Dressing:
To Be or Not to Be?

Salad dressings don't know whether they are emulsions or not; let's make one and see why. (Makes about 1 cup or 240 mL).

You need:

mixing jar with lid

1 teaspoon (5 mL) herbs
  (chopped parsley,
  chives, mint, tarragon,
  or a combination)

$3/4$ cup (180 mL) oil

$1/4$ cup (60 mL) vinegar

salt and pepper to taste

WHAT TO DO:

Place all the ingredients in the jar and shake well. Store in refrigerator, and shake before using.

WHAT HAPPENS:

When shaken, the vinegar and oil combine, but then they eventually separate.

WHY:

The vinegar, oil, and water are a *temporary* emulsion or colloid, of small molecular substances that combine temporarily with other small molecular substances in a liquid. Salad dressing is not a true emulsion, as mayonnaise is, or it would not separate.

· ·

Endothermic Frozen Treat: Cranberry Lemon Snow

Can an endothermic change, or one where heat energy is used instead of produced, make a delicious frozen treat? In **Ice Bound** (page 90) we froze plain water, but now let's try fruit and lemon juice. You'll have the fun of doing this great chemistry experiment and eating it, too!

You need:

small, clean jar

$1/_2$ cup (120 mL) cranberry
  or other fruit juice

1 tablespoon (15 mL) lemon juice

medium-size mixing bowl
  or container

6 cups crushed ice (see page 91)

$1/_2$ cup (120 mL) rock salt
  (available in spice section
  of supermarket)

sheets of paper towels
  or 2 small dish towels
  (to fold and wrap around bowl)

WHAT TO DO:

Pour the fruit juice and the lemon juice into the jar and shake. Place the open jar in the middle of the bowl. Carefully pour crushed ice around the jar up to the top. Sprinkle rock salt in and around the ice. Fold the paper towels or dish towels lengthwise and wrap them around the bowl. Place a heavy object or two against the bowl to keep the towels in place. Be patient! It will take about two hours for your experiment to turn into an icy treat.

WHAT HAPPENS:

The juice turns into an icy slush.

WHY:

The salt on the ice draws the heat out of the juices in the jar and the temperature goes down below the freezing point.

I Scream!

Endotherm another frozen treat by replacing the Cranberry Lemon Snow juices with 1 tablespoon (15 mL) instant vanilla pudding powder, $1/4$ cup (60 mL) chilled evaporated milk, $1/2$ cup (120 mL) low-fat milk, 1 tablespoon (15 mL) sugar, and $1/2$ teaspoon (2 mL) vanilla extract. Mix the ingredients thoroughly before packing the open jar in ice. It's a delicious soft-serve vanilla ice cream.

Maple Snow Sugar

Early colonists in America made a special maple candy called "Jack Wax." Boiled maple syrup was poured onto the snow and hardened into a sugary maple treat. You can make your own Jack Wax in just a few minutes.

You need:
microwave-safe container
$1/_2$ cup (120 mL) pure maple syrup
use of microwave
spoon
medium bowl half-filled
  with crushed ice

fork

WHAT TO DO:
Pour the syrup into the microwave-safe container. Cook on high power for five minutes. Very carefully (hot sugar can cause a bad burn), spoon the maple syrup over the crushed ice.

WHAT HAPPENS:
The hot syrup turns into strands of taffylike maple candy. With the fork, you can now pick out strands of taffylike maple sugar and roll it into hard balls. Enjoy them alone, as a morning treat with doughnuts, or with delicious sparkling apple cider pancakes in **Batter on the Moon** (page 115).

WHY:
The maple syrup, boiled to the hard-sugar stage, is chemically changed so that the individual sugar crystals link up and harden together to form a solid.

Batter on the Moon (HOT!)

No, they don't play baseball on the moon but you can make light, delicious, sparkling apple cider pancakes that are guaranteed to be out of this world! The chemically changed mixed batter, with its bubbles and holes, will remind you of craters on the moon. You won't strike out with this experiment if you keep your eyes on the batter. (Makes 16 four-inch pancakes.)

You need:

mixing bowl

2 cups (280 g) baking and
  pancake mix, such as Bisquick

$1^1/_3$ cups (320 mL)
  sparkling (apple) cider

1 egg

pancake turner

$1/_2$ cup (120 mL) oil,
  plus extra for pan

wire whisk or mixing spoon

measuring cup with spout

electric fry pan, or regular
  frying pan and use of stove

WHAT TO DO:

Pour the pancake mix, cider, eggs, and $1/_2$ cup (120 ml) oil into the bowl and mix them together with the wire whisk or spoon. Do not overmix. Pour the batter into the measuring cup.

Lightly grease the pan or electric fry pan (set at 350°F). When the pan is hot, start the pancakes by pouring the batter into the pan. Pour enough to make 4- or 5-inch (10–13 cm) pancakes. Let the pancakes cook on one side until bubbles appear and until the surface is somewhat dry. Turn the pancakes over with the turner and cook until pancakes lightly lift from pan.

WHAT HAPPENS:

As you mix the batter, bubbles appear in it. When you add heat, cooking the batter, it turns into light delicious pancakes. Serve them with butter, syrup, and applesauce. Adding our Maple Snow candies (see previous recipe) would make this breakfast an even bigger hit.

WHY:

The apple juice in cider is carbonated, or creates carbonic acid. This happens when carbon dioxide is dissolved into the solution. The craters, or holes in the pancake batter are created by the carbon dioxide, which is a gas. This also makes the pancakes lighter and fluffier. If you save leftover batter for later, the pancakes will be heavier and flatter, because the carbon dioxide bubbles will lessen or disappear. This is similar to when you put uncapped soda in the refrigerator and it loses its fizz.

THE LAB:
CO$_2$ AND YOU

In this chapter, you'll make a manometer, an exciting and great piece of chemistry equipment to put in your laboratory, a place where you, as chief chemist, will be doing your own research and studies. A manometer is easy and inexpensive to make and fun to use. With it you'll be able to test substances for the gas carbon dioxide (CO$_2$).

But first, it's time to solve the mystery of the rising doughs and find out which contains the most CO$_2$.

Dynamite Dumplings (HOT!)

What substances added to flour and water produce the most carbon dioxide (CO_2)? In this three-part experiment you'll make a water and flour dough three times, using a different combination of substances.

Each part of the experiment will be done separately, using the same equipment and ingredients, almost. The only thing to change will be the substance to be tested: baking powder, baking soda, or quick-rising dry yeast. Before you start, make a hypothesis, or scientific guess, as to which substance contains the most carbon dioxide. Then do the tests and find out if you are right.

You need:

small cup or mug

tablespoon

flour

test substances:

  $1/2$ tablespoon (7.5 mL) baking powder

  $1/2$ tablespoon (7.5 mL) baking soda

  $1/2$ tablespoon (7.5 mL) quick-rising dry yeast

cool water

cup filled with very hot water

use of stove or microwave

WHAT TO DO:

With a teaspoon, mix a full tablespoon (15 mL) of dry flour with the first test substance, the baking powder, in a cup or mug. Add a little bit of cool water, a drop at a time, and make a ball of dough. If the mixture becomes too wet, add more flour. Place the ball of dough in a tablespoon. Leave the spoon in a cool place while you fill another cup or mug with very hot water (from the tap, or warmed on the stove or in a microwave).

For about two minutes, hold the spoon with the dough over the hot water. Let the spoon touch the water, and a little of the hot water enter it. Set the ball of dough aside.

Now, repeat the experiment, but instead of the baking powder use baking soda. Then do the experiment again with the third substance, the quick-rising yeast.

WHAT HAPPENS:

All the dough balls grow much larger.

WHY:

The baking powder contains bicarbonate of soda. When combined with flour, water, and heat, it creates a chemical change that produces carbon dioxide. This is seen in the gas-bubble holes that appear in the dough and make it larger. The baking soda and the yeast doughs also produce chemical changes and CO_2. The baking soda dough will probably grow less than the baking powder and yeast doughs, which may even double in size. Of the two, the yeast dough should grow slightly larger. Was your hypothesis correct?

Make Your Own Manometer

Your manometer is simply a plastic tube pushed down inside a glass bottle with the other end attached to a stick. You'll use it to test different substances for carbon dioxide and have the fun of watching the colored water rise in the plastic tube, somewhat like a thermometer. You can even calibrate, or put lines on, your tube-stick with a marking pen to measure, and record, how much gas is in a substance. If the colored water shoots up the tube or even comes out of it, you'll know the test substance produces a lot of carbon dioxide.

You need:

16 ounce (473 mL) glass bottle
  with a screw-on cap

large nail and hammer

28 inches (71 cm)
  of standard plastic tubing

modeling clay

wide-mouth jar lid

marking pen

stick about 16 inches
  (40 cm) long

rubber bands or twist ties

small glass half-filled with water

food coloring (any color)

medicine dropper

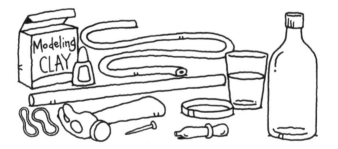

WHAT TO DO:

Clean the bottle thoroughly. Have an adult make a large hole in the bottle cap with the nail and hammer. (Make sure the hole is wide enough for the tube to pass through.) Push about 4

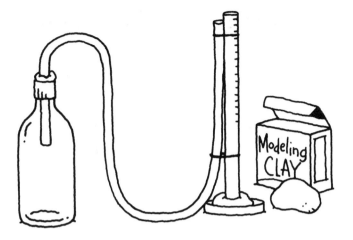

inches (10 cm) of the 28 inches (71 cm) of tubing through the hole in the cap, into the bottle. (Bend the tube back and forth to straighten it.) Make a small clay rope and press it around the hole in the top to make the bottle airtight. Now take the jar lid and press clay into the bottom of it; put a little more in the middle.

At this point, you may wish to draw some measurement lines on the stick with a marking pen. Each line should be one centimeter from the next, starting from the middle of the stick to one end. Number the lines, starting with 1 in the middle. This makes a nice scale and lets you know how much each substance causes your manometer to register.

Now, push the stick into the clay-filled lid so that it stands up. Bend the outside tubing to the bottom of the bottle and stand to form a lower loop and fasten the rest of the tubing to the stick with the rubber bands. The tube opening should be at the top of the stick. You are now ready to fill the lower loop with colored water.

Put a few drops of food coloring in the half-glass of water to color it. With the medicine dropper, drop one or two drops of colored water into the top of the tube on the stick. If the water separates in the tube, gently suck or blow on the straw to bring the water drops together. You now have a new piece of chemistry equipment to use in your lab experiments.

The Care and Use of Your Manometer

1. Work on a kitchen counter, in case water spills out of the top of your manometer.

2. Keep extra colored water in a small closed bottle, to replace any water lost during experiments or storage.

3. When taking the top off the manometer bottle to add solutions, place the tube with the lid on it into another similar empty bottle so that the colored water in the tube won't escape or break up.

4. So as not to twist the tube and loosen the seal, screw the bottle into the cap instead of the cap onto the bottle.

5. Store your manometer in a small box. Make certain the cap with the tube in it is screwed tightly on the bottle.

6. Drop only one or two drops of colored water into the top of the plastic tube on the stick. If the water breaks up, gently blow and suck into the plastic tube. The colored water should come back together.

7. To do tests, pour powders first, followed by liquids, into your manometer bottle and cap it immediately. Your experiments will not work if you mix the solutions in other containers and then pour them into the manometer bottle, or if you do not close the bottle quickly enough.

Get a Lift From CO₂

How much will the colored-water marker rise when certain substances are placed on the manometer? Whether you do these manometer experiments on one day or on several days, it is very important to keep a scientific journal, or record book, and write down what happens in each and every experiment. Doing and recording these experiments will make a real chemist out of you.

You need:

manometer

medicine dropper

colored water

empty spare bottle

test substance:

1 tablespoon (15 mL) baking powder and $1/4$ cup (60 mL) vinegar

WHAT TO DO:

Set up your manometer on the kitchen counter or with newspaper under the container to catch any spills. Keep the bottle and stand close together so the tube makes a low loop between them. With the dropper, place one or two drops of colored water in the open tube attached to the stand. Only a few drops are needed! The water should drop down into the lower loop.

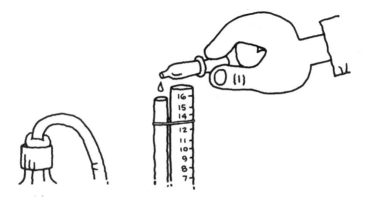

If it does not do this, or if it breaks up, gently blow or suck on the tube to bring the liquid together and move it into place in the lower loop.

Now measure out the baking powder and vinegar. Take the cap off the manometer bottle and rest the tube in another bottle. Pour the baking powder into the bottom of the manometer bottle, followed by the vinegar (the liquid always goes in last). Quickly screw the cap back on tightly and shake the bottle a little. Write down what happens and how far the solution makes the colored-water marker rise in the tube.

Wash out the manometer bottle thoroughly before going on to the next experiment, and remember to wash it again between experiments or you might invalidate, or spoil, your results.

Now test the next five combinations as you did the baking powder and vinegar experiment:

Test substances:

1 tablespoon (15 mL) baking soda and $1/_4$ cup (60 mL) vinegar

2 antacid seltzer tablets (such as Alka-Seltzer) and $1/_2$ cup (120 mL) water

$1/_2$ cup (120 mL) carbonated soft drink

1 tablespoon (15 mL) baking soda and juice of one lemon

1 tablespoon (15 mL) baking soda and $1/_3$ cup (80 mL) water.

NOTE: For added experiment effects and results, try varying, or changing, the amounts of dry ingredients to liquids, and of different liquids to powders.

WHAT HAPPENS:

The colored water in the manometer top rises forcefully up the tube with much sputtering and bubbling, or it rises slightly but does not sputter, or it does not rise at all.

WHY:

There is obviously more CO_2 given off in some chemical reactions than in others. In the above experiments, both vinegar-and-baking-soda and vinegar-and-baking-powder produced the best results. Both mixtures drove the colored-water marker bubbling noisily up the tube.*

While there was definitely some CO_2 given off with the seltzer tablets, soda, and baking-soda-and-lemon solutions, the water marker did not move as much as it did with the powder and vinegar solutions. In these tests, there was little movement and no noticeable sound. But absolutely nothing happened with the baking-soda-and-water solutions, which released no CO_2 at all.

*If you did not get this reaction, do the experiments again. Be sure to put the powder in first, and to cap the bottle quickly before the CO_2 gas being released can escape.

INDEX